D0088330

H. RICHARD NIEBUHR

A Lifetime of Reflections on the Church and the World

Dr. Richard Niebuhr
(Alfred Eisenstaedt, *Life Magazine,* © 1955 Time Inc.)

H. RICHARD NIEBUHR

A Lifetime of Reflections on the Church and the World

Jon Diefenthaler

MERCER
UNIVERSITY PRESS

ISBN 0-86554-214-7

H. Richard Niebuhr
A Lifetime of Reflections on the Church and the World

Mercer University Press, Macon, Georgia 31207

Printed in the United States of America

The paper used in this publication meets the minimum requirements of American National Standard for Information Sciences— Permanence of Paper for Printed Library Materials, ANSI Z39.48-1984.

Library of Congress Cataloging-in-Publication Data

Diefenthaler, Jon.
H. Richard Niebuhr : a lifetime of reflections on the church and the world.

Includes bibliographical references and index.
1. Niebuhr, H. Richard (Helmut Richard), 1894–1962.
I. Title.
BX4827.N47D54 1986 230′.092′4 86-14361
ISBN 0-86554-214-7 (alk. paper)
ISBN 0-86554-235-X (pbk. : alk. paper)

Contents

to
Linda Reineck Diefenthaler

Reinhold and Richard Niebuhr upon graduation from Eden Seminary
(Courtesy Eden Theological Seminary Archives)

PREFACE

The Man and the Scholar

Born on 3 September 1894 in Wright City, Missouri, Helmut Richard was the youngest member of the devout and gifted Niebuhr family. His father, Gustav Niebuhr, had emigrated to the United States from Germany in 1878 and became a stalwart pastor in the German Evangelical Synod of North America, serving congregations in San Francisco, Wright City and Saint Charles, Missouri, and finally Lincoln, Illinois. His mother, Lydia Hosto Niebuhr, had been born in America of German immigrant parents. Her father was another Evangelical pastor with whom Gustav Niebuhr was closely associated in the San Francisco area. A very warm, expressive person, she showed a deep love for music and literature and proved to be a gifted artist. In addition to their two other sons, Walter and Reinhold, the Niebuhrs had a daughter, Hulda, who became a professor of Christian education at McCormick Theological Seminary in Chicago. Walter, on the other hand, stood out because he chose "business" as his career. Reinhold Niebuhr taught at Union Theological Seminary in New York City, where he became one of the twentieth century's best-known religious leaders.

Like his father and brother Reinhold before him, Richard Niebuhr decided to enter the ministry of the Evangelical Synod. He enrolled at that denomination's Elmhurst College at age fourteen and completed four years of pre-seminary training in 1912. He then went on to Eden Theological Seminary in Saint Louis, graduating in 1915. A year later he was ordained as the minister of Walnut Park Evangelical Church in north Saint Louis.

Yet it was primarily in higher education that this Niebuhr served his denomination. In 1919 he joined the Eden faculty. He left in 1922 to do graduate work at Yale Divinity School, where he completed the requirements for both a B.D. and a Ph.D. in 1924. He then became president of Elmhurst College, and by 1927 succeeded in setting the college on the road to becoming a strong liberal arts school. In the fall of 1927 he returned to Eden Seminary as academic dean, a position he held for the next four years. During that time he directed the preliminary negotiations that led to the eventual "union" of the

Evangelical Synod with the German Reformed church and completed his first published book, *The Social Sources of Denominationalism.* In 1930 he spent his sabbatical traveling and studying in Europe. Soon after his return in 1931 he accepted the invitation to become associate professor of Christian ethics at Yale Divinity School.

These early years illuminate Richard Niebuhr's personality and piety. From his father he took his physical features, but his temperament was more like his mother's. Former colleagues and close friends still remember him as an extremely sensitive and essentially private person who approached other people and his work in a self-effacing manner. The Niebuhr family seems to have supplied both incentive for scholarly pursuits and a setting that nurtured a deep, personal devotion to Christianity. Among its members, piety and intellect were never incompatible. Throughout Richard Niebuhr's career, the Bible was a consistent frame of reference, and he sprinkled his rhetoric with the words of Jesus, the Old Testament prophets, and Saint Paul. Even after he left the Evangelical Synod to teach at Yale, he still made it a practice to open his classes with prayers that students often sought to publish; and he was frequently the faculty member favored to deliver the invocation for opening or commencement services.

Though both men were widely respected among intellectuals, Richard Niebuhr did not achieve as much public recognition as his brother Reinhold. Like Reinhold, Richard set forth a bold theological response to the mounting political upheavals occasioned by the Great Depression and World War II. Drawing on the more classical understanding of the Christian faith that neoorthodoxy had helped revive in America, he summoned the church to take a more prophetic stand in the world. But clearly it was Reinhold who went on to receive the greater acclaim, flamboyantly championing the cause of social justice and assuming formal leadership roles in religious and political circles. Richard did not enjoy and so avoided this kind of limelight. He preferred to exercise his influence in a more informal and quiet way. The brothers' youth provides an analogy. While growing up in their father's midwestern parsonage, each chose a different musical instrument to play in the family ensemble—Reinhold, the trombone, and Richard, the flute. Their choice may have been merely coincidental, but it seems to have presaged the contrasting styles of the two brothers.[1]

At the same time Richard and Reinhold Niebuhr showed remarkably similar attitudes toward their denomination. Both clearly shared a common commitment to the classical Reformation theology of sin and grace that all members

---

[1]See Liston Pope, "H. Richard Niebuhr: A Personal Appreciation," in *Faith and Ethics: The Theology of H. Richard Niebuhr,* ed. Paul Ramsey (New York, 1957) 4-5.

of the Evangelical Synod were taught to treasure and defend. Niebuhr scholars have tended to focus on the theological differences that subsequently arose between the two during their public debate over the Manchurian crisis of 1932. But in matters concerning their church, the brothers frequently pulled together and worked effectively as a team. Their goal was to hasten its acculturation, to expand the scope of its social concern, and to strengthen its base through union with other denominations.

From 1931 until his death on 5 July 1962 Yale Divinity School was the center of Richard Niebuhr's life. He was elevated to the rank of full professor in 1938, to Director of Graduate Studies in Religion in 1953, and shortly thereafter, to the prestigious post of Sterling Professor. Yet none of this recognition took precedence over his concern for students and the churchly vocations for which he was preparing them. As a faculty member, Niebuhr scrupulously observed the counseling duties assigned to him and never stopped revising his annual course in "Christian Ethics." This commitment to the church set him apart from his brother Reinhold. Looking back on the decade of the Great Depression, the younger Niebuhr recalled that, whereas his brother had assumed the responsibility to reform his culture, the "special task" to which he felt called was the reformation of the church.[2] In 1956 he published *The Purpose of the Church and Its Ministry.* The book was in fact a byproduct of his decision to postpone all other scholarly research and to serve as director of an intensive investigation of theological education in church seminaries and divinity schools all across the American continent.

Always paramount in Niebuhr's thinking were the concepts of "church" and "world." As early as 1929 his purpose in treating the plurality of American religious bodies in *Social Sources* was not so much to describe denominational divisions as to awaken Christians to their sad consequences. The eyesore, as he saw it, was the tendency for whole denominations to accommodate themselves to humanity's divisions into classes, races, and nations. This prevented the development of a Christianity capable of integrating America's culture. In 1935 he helped write *The Church Against the World,* a work in which he openly attacked the liberal Protestant tendency to fuse Christianity with culture. Two years later Niebuhr succeeded in organizing three hundred years of history around the theme, *The Kingdom of God in America.* He used the concept of "movement" to explain the dynamics of Protestant Christianity's development and transmission. The book did not receive the acclaim it deserved until much

---

[2]H. Richard Niebuhr, "Reformation: Continuing Imperative," *Christian Century* 77 (2 March 1960): 248-51.

later, when a new generation of religious historians helped awaken a fresh concern over the role of theology in the shaping of American culture.[3]

Niebuhr developed this same theme in two other major books. The first of these is perhaps his best-known work, *Christ and Culture*. Published in 1951, the book outlined five distinct types of Christian attitudes toward the world. Between the two extremes of "withdrawal" (Christ against culture) and "identification" (Christ of culture), Niebuhr placed three mediating attitudes: the "synthesist" (Christ above culture), the "dualist" (Christ and culture in paradox), and the "conversionist" (Christ the transformer of culture). To the representatives of the first of these mediating attitudes, most notably Thomas Aquinas, Christ was both the fulfillment of a culture's aspirations and the restorer of its society, but only in a preliminary fashion. "True culture" still needed Christ to enter life "from above" with supernatural gifts that directed persons toward the right center of value. The second, dualistic Christianity, viewed Christians as citizens of two worlds and subject to twin moralities. According to its Lutheran proponents, the dual authorities of Christ and culture were in opposition to each other; this view demanded obedience to both authorities and authorized Christians to "sin boldly" in the hope of a justification that lay beyond this world. Finally, the "conversionist" view regarded the world as corrupt; yet it was still the arena of God's creative and ordering activity. Among its representatives (Augustine, Calvin, Jonathan Edwards), Christ became a transformer of culture. He consistently turned persons and their societies away from self to God, but always within the framework of culture. These categories remain important points of reference for scholars seeking to explain the church's behavior in any society or period of history. The other book, *Radical Monotheism and Western Culture* (1960), contained a tightly woven analysis of the henotheistic and polytheistic forms of faith Niebuhr saw at work within all of Western civilization. He argued that both were perversions of monotheistic trust and loyalty to God because they either attempted to make a god out of the culture itself or else gave devotion to one or more of its political, scientific, or religious features.

This book represents an effort to call attention to Niebuhr's lifelong struggle to express the church's proper relationship to the world. Several scholars have noted the centrality of this theme. Libertus A. Hoedemaker, for instance, asserts that in one way or another, all of Niebuhr's thought figures around "the

---

[3]See William A. Clebsch, "A New Historiography of American Religion," *Historical Magazine of the Protestant Episcopal Church* 32 (September 1963): 225-57; Henry F. May, "The Recovery of American Religious History," *American Historical Review* 70 (October 1964): 79-92; Paul A. Carter, "Recent Historiography of Protestant Churches in America," *Church History* 27 (March 1968): 95-107.

relation between the gospel and the culture to which it belongs and in which it functions." In his estimation, Niebuhr's concern was not the metaphysics of God, but always the conversion of the individual and of his life in society.[4] "To a remarkable degree," writes John D. Godsey, Niebuhr's thinking stayed at "the cutting edge between the Christian faith and the world of unbelief, at times calling the church to defend the substance of its faith against the world and at other times demanding that the church engage the world for the sake of its mission, but at all times keeping church and world in dialogue with one another."[5]

My own assessment of Niebuhr goes one step further. I not only see the "dialogue" at every point in Niebuhr's works, but find that this important scholar's church background and response to the world of his day shed considerable light on the entire process of its development. The first chapter, reflecting Niebuhr's student days and early leadership in the Evangelical Synod, highlights his various attempts to combat his denomination's isolation from the culture of the United States. This experience not only contributed directly to the perspective he brought to bear on immigrant groups like his own, but sharpened his aversion to the worldly aspects of the church. At various points in *Social Sources,* Niebuhr was also advocating a strategy of "withdrawal." Chapter two highlights his concern for the theological issues facing Protestantism in general during the 1930s and traces the path along which he continued to search for a framework capable of keeping lively and taut the tension between "church" and "world." His response to the Great Depression not only strengthened his determination to set the church against the world but deepened his commitment to the social gospel. Not surprisingly, both of these themes appear in *The Kingdom of God in America.*

Both chapters underscore the close relationship between Niebuhr's personal and intellectual life. Unfortunately, this relationship cannot be studied as intensively after he left Eden Seminary in 1931. While a substantial collection of material, consisting chiefly of his unpublished essays, sermons, and lectures, has been preserved,[6] almost all of his correspondence from the three decades he spent at Yale seems to have been either discarded or destroyed. One can only speculate at this point, but it appears that this intensely private man, who was at times plagued by self-doubt and depression, wanted to draw the curtain around the more personal side of his life. Niebuhr friends and family, more-

---

[4]Libertus A. Hoedemaker, *The Theology of H. Richard Niebuhr* (Philadelphia, 1970) xvii.

[5]John D. Godsey, *The Promise of H. Richard Niebuhr* (Philadelphia, 1970) 18.

[6]This collection remains in the custody of Richard R. Niebuhr at the Harvard Divinity School, Cambridge MA.

over, seem reluctant or unable to bridge much of this tragic gap in his biography.

What *is* known of Richard Niebuhr's life adds considerable perspective to his theological development. Most of his interpreters agree that he worked out his thinking in response to public events and personal experiences. Yet they have tended to restrict themselves to the philosophical and theological aspects of his work. Hoedemaker's *Theology of H. Richard Niebuhr,* for instance, is a critical analysis of some of his major ideas in the light of recent theological trends in Europe and the United States. This is also true of the two most comprehensive studies to date, James W. Fowler's *To See the Kingdom: The Theological Vision of H. Richard Niebuhr* and Lonnie D. Kliever's *H. Richard Niebuhr,* as well as of Godsey's *Promise of H. Richard Niebuhr,* and Jerry A. Irish's *The Religious Thought of H. Richard Niebuhr,* the most recent.[7]

These writers, except Fowler, also have paid scant attention to his upbringing and career in the Evangelical Synod. The common practice, or so it appears, is to draw on his article of 1960 in the "How My Mind Has Changed" series of the *Christian Century,* accepting without challenge his hindsight that the 1930s formed the "decisive period" in the formulation of his convictions, and tracing the emergence of his ethical theology from this point.[8] The early chapters of this book should make plain the importance of Niebuhr's early years for evaluating any "change" in his perspective. Against this backdrop, his theology appears to have evolved gradually. The emphasis Niebuhr placed on a God-centered faith during the thirties was not merely a product of the "neoorthodox" ferment. That ferment served more as a catalyst, activating and strengthening convictions that had taken shape during his formative years in the Evangelical Synod.

The third and fourth chapters keep the focus on the rich interplay between Niebuhr's thinking and major events of the 1940s and 1950s. Like the Great Depression, the outbreak of World War II in Europe and the inability of the churches to address America's preoccupation with its own defense and self-interested policies intensified his emphasis on Christianity's prophetic role in a democratic society. Neither Pearl Harbor nor subsequent victories over the Axis powers in Europe and the Far East served to alter this concern for American life. Yet in the process there were obvious refinements in Niebuhr's reflections on "church" and "world" as he moved in the direction of the

---

[7]In addition to Hoedemaker and Godsey, see James W. Fowler, *To See the Kingdom: The Theological Vision of H. Richard Niebuhr* (Nashville, 1974); Lonnie D. Kliever, *H. Richard Niebuhr* (Waco TX, 1977); and Jerry A. Irish, *The Religious Thought of H. Richard Niebuhr* (Atlanta, 1985).

[8]H. Richard Niebuhr, "Reformation: Continuing Imperative."

"conversionist" approach he set forth in *Christ and Culture.* During the 1950s, as the nation was swept by a "return to religion," he in fact attempted to integrate the new insights into a vision of church renewal that he hoped would expedite the transformation of America's culture.

Thanks are due to many individuals who were immensely helpful at various stages in this study. Insights into America's religious history learned from Sidney E. Mead at the University of Iowa stimulated the interest in writing a doctoral dissertation on Richard Niebuhr. Ellis W. Hawley provided valuable criticisms and editorial assistance. Lowell Zuck of Eden Theological Seminary, the late Robert C. Stenger at Elmhurst College, and Richard R. Niebuhr of the Harvard Divinity School were gracious enough to permit the use of unpublished Niebuhr materials. William G. Chrystal also shared bibliographical sources and gave encouragement. Timothy L. Smith made possible a year of postdoctoral work in the department of history at The Johns Hopkins University and guided the process of revising the manuscript into a form suitable for publication. Linda Jones, Judy Meier, and Mary Brandes served most ably and efficiently as typists. The American Society of Church History granted permission to adapt some of the material for chapters one and two which appeared in *Church History* 52 (June 1983): 172-85 as "H. Richard Niebuhr: A Fresh Look at His Early Years." Deepest feelings of gratitude go to my wife, Linda Reineck Diefenthaler, for all that she both sacrificed and provided during the time required to prepare this study, and to our children, Andrew, Katie, Lisa, and Heidi, who so patiently waited for the day when their father would have more time for them than he did for H. Richard Niebuhr.

H. Richard Niebuhr, 1924
(Courtesy Richard R. Niebuhr)

CHAPTER I

The Evangelical Synod and the New World of America

"Denominationalism . . . represents the moral failure of Christianity."

H. Richard Niebuhr
Social Sources of Denominationalism, 25

In his preface to *The Social Sources of Denominationalism,* H. Richard Niebuhr gave his reasons for undertaking the book. A course in "Symbolics" he taught as a seminary professor had convinced him that any attempt to distinguish denominations primarily by references to their doctrines or to approach the problem of Christian unity from a purely theological point of view was "artificial and fruitless." Real understanding required a shift of orientation from theology to history, sociology, and ethics.[1]

Such a rationale, however, does not explain what follows in the body of the work. For as his chapters unfold, the author's urgent sense of purpose becomes apparent. His historical and sociological appraisals do not mask his personal frustration over the divided character of Christendom. His descriptions of denominationalism as an "evil," an "unacknowledged hypocrisy," and a "compromise" of Christian ideals convey deep anger at the general condition of the church in America. Few indictments could have been more bitter than his judgment that denominations represented "the accommodation of Christianity to the caste system of human society." The "division," he declared, "draws the color line in the church of God; it fosters the misunderstandings, the self-exaltations, the hatreds of jingoistic nationalism by continuing in the body of Christ the spurious differences of provincial loyalties; it seats the rich and poor apart at the table of the Lord, where the fortunate may enjoy the bounty that

[1]H. Richard Niebuhr (hereafter cited as HRN), *The Social Sources of Denominationalism* (New York, 1929) vii.

they have provided while the others feed upon the crusts their poverty affords."[2] *Social Sources* was in fact a passionate plea for Christian unity.

1

Helping to shape his attitude was Niebuhr's experience in the Evangelical Synod of North America. To a large extent, *Social Sources* mirrors his ambivalence toward the ethnic features of that denomination and the difficulties attending its movement into the cultural mainstream following World War I. Niebuhr remained a loyal son, embracing the faith his ancestors had bequeathed to him; but for that faith to have an influence on American culture and to give direction to its people, he was convinced that denominations like his own needed to assume a more ecumenical stance both toward the world and toward other denominations.

Comparatively small (about a quarter of a million members during Niebuhr's day), the Evangelical Synod had historical roots that extended back to the Reformation in Germany. Its European forebears did not form an identifiable group, however, until 1817, when King Frederich Wilhelm III brought together Lutheran and Reformed pastors and congregations in the "Prussian Union." At that point the "Evangelicals" stood out because of their wholehearted acceptance of the "Union." Later, more for political or economic than for religious reasons, a number of them emigrated to America. In 1840 the immigrants organized the *Deutscher Evangelische Kirchenverein des Westens*. In 1866 they chose the Americanized name of "German Evangelical Synod of North America," the name by which they were known until 1925, when the word *German* was dropped. Membership, always drawn chiefly from newly arrived German Lutheran and Reformed elements in the Midwest, soon became concentrated in the Saint Louis area and in southern Illinois, although large parishes were also developed in cities like Chicago, Milwaukee, and Detroit.

While their theological heritage largely stemmed from Luther, and to a lesser extent from Zwingli and Calvin, the founders of Niebuhr's denomination were also influenced by the spirit of the pietist missionaries sent to serve them by various societies in Europe, especially those headquartered at Basel, Barmen, and Bremen. Among these early Evangelicals, religion became more a matter of the "heart" than the "head." Under the primitive conditions of the American frontier, such inclinations helped to mold the synod's resistance to formalized subscription to confessional creeds, its emphasis on an experimental type of faith, and its warm concern for the physical and spiritual welfare of both society and the individual.

This legacy of pietism, when coupled with the ancestry of a "union" church, caused Evangelicals to seek closer ties with other Christians in America. Within

---

[2]Ibid., 6.

the first generation, the synod merged with such bodies as the German Evangelical Church Society of Ohio, the United Evangelical Synod of the Northwest, and the United Evangelical Synod of the East. The synod also exchanged fraternal delegates with the Presbyterian and Congregational churches, and it gave active support to such interdenominational organizations as the Evangelical Alliance, the American Tract and Bible societies, and the American Home Missionary Society. In 1934 it united with the Reformed Church in the United States, which then numbered over 600,000 members. This new organization, known as The Evangelical and Reformed Church, merged in 1957 with the Congregational Christian Churches to become today's United Church of Christ.

Historians of the Evangelical Synod have tended to see it as one of the more ecumenical members of the larger family of German Protestants. When its founders formed their organization in 1848, Carl Schneider points out, they made it at first a *Kirchenverein,* an informal "society" rather than a formal synod. They did not want denominational distinctions to impede their efforts to meet the needs of German immigrants of Lutheran and Reformed backgrounds. Schneider also isolates a passage in which Niebuhr's forebears in the Evangelical Synod set forth their philosophy.

> We recognize the Evangelical church as that communion which acknowledges the Holy Scriptures of the Old and New Testament as the Word of God and as the sole and infallible rule of faith and life, and accepts the interpretation of the Holy Scriptures as given in the symbolic books of the Lutheran *and* the Reformed Church, the most important being: The Augsburg Confession, Luther's and the Heidelberg Catechisms, *in so far as they agree;* but where they disagree, we adhere strictly to the passages of Holy Scripture bearing on the subject, and avail ourselves of the liberty of conscience prevailing in the Evangelical Church.[3]

According to Louis W. Goebel, an Evangelical pastor and close personal friend of Niebuhr's who later became president of the Evangelical and Reformed church, the synod from its beginning desired to be known as a "united and a uniting fellowship." In later years, the slogan "only Evangelical" served notice to everyone that the denomination "refused to be bound by rigid confessional statements."[4]

Up until World War I, however, a strong desire to preserve and to transmit the synod's "Germanness" tended to check these ecumenical impulses. As new immigrants kept coming, Evangelical congregations continued to use

---

[3]Carl E. Schneider, *The German Church on the American Frontier* (St. Louis, 1939) 409 (italics added).

[4]Louis W. Goebel, *Recollections* (n.p., 1959) 85.

German liturgies in worship, to operate parochial schools according to the German pattern, and to require that catechetical training prior to confirmation be conducted in the German tongue. Almost every Evangelical clergyman, known locally as "the German minister," could function with little or no knowledge of English. Close ties with the "Union" church in Germany, moreover, seemed to uphold the trend. It was from Germany, for example, that the synod's Eden Seminary took its academic standards, most of its faculty, and nearly half of its students. In 1892 Eden requested permission from the synod to appoint a professor to teach classes in English, but was turned down because the synod's board of directors felt that there were not enough ministers to supply the vacant German-speaking congregations of the synod, which they believed had to be served first. So at the seminary, only students were capable of conducting "English" classes.[5]

Among the Evangelicals who took exception to the exclusiveness of the synod's "German" behavior were the Niebuhr family. Richard Niebuhr's father, Gustav, publicly chided his church for failing to recognize that its mission under the gospel of Christ was "to exercise a direct and wholesome influence" on "all social and political conditions" of the human race. "Existing conditions would be different," he told the members of his denomination in 1913, "if the Churches, instead of watching over their small denominational differences and over their often still smaller local business affairs, had with concerted action applied their influence to the vital needs of society in a way that could not be misunderstood." Whenever it came to "the question of remedying municipal and social evils of any kind," he thought, "little denominational bickerings should not count." In such cases there should be "decided concerted action of all who hold to the Christian standard of righteousness."[6] That same year Gustav Niebuhr died after a diabetes attack, but his vision lived on in his sons, Reinhold and Richard.

At the time of their father's death, the brothers were both attending Eden Seminary. Reinhold Niebuhr was two academic years ahead of Richard and tended to be the more dominant figure on campus. The younger Niebuhr displayed his talent as a budding poet in *The Keryx,* a journal published five times

---

[5]See Carl E. Schneider, *History of the Theological Seminary of the Evangelical Church* (n.p., 1925) 12, 39-40, 43. Schneider also notes that of the 65 students enrolled at the seminary in 1890-1891, thirty had come from Germany or Switzerland. And in 1900, when Eden celebrated its fiftieth anniversary, its board chairman received a congratulatory message from the German emperor himself.

[6]Gustav Niebuhr, "In What Way and to What Extent Should the Church Exercise Influence on Social and Political Conditions?" *The Messenger of Peace* 12 (15 May 1913): 2, and ibid. (1 June 1913): 1-2. For biographical material on Gustav Niebuhr, see William G. Chrystal, *A Father's Mantle: The Legacy of Gustav Niebuhr* (New York, 1982).

a year by Eden's students. "Winter Peace," his first published work, appeared in 1912. The poem clearly communicated the naiveté of an eighteen-year-old nestled in the embrace of his "German" denomination.[7] Two years later *The Keryx* published his second effort, "Youth." Niebuhr wrote,

My life is strong with the strength of years,
That were and are to be;
My soul is bold with the vanquished fears
And the victories I shall see.[8]

World War I would soon shatter such optimism for many young intellectuals, but in 1914 Niebuhr seemed to have had little inkling of the difficult days that the war would bring upon the world and the church of his youth. In fact, none of his later writings radiate such a triumphal mood.

These earliest literary efforts did enable Niebuhr to cultivate his facility for the English language. At Eden Niebuhr found it confusing to be an American who was still required to speak "German." As a student critic of one of his papers pointed out, he tended to distort the English language with Germanisms. Instead of "such a singer is *rightfully* called," Niebuhr had written "such a singer is called *with right*."[9] He became determined to overcome the cultural handicap. While interest in writing poetry faded, the prose with which he graced his published writings was always highly polished and was often perfected to the point of eloquence.

Like his brother Reinhold, Richard believed that the Evangelical Synod was embarrassingly out of step with the march of life in America. At Elmhurst, a school for pretheological students patterned after the German *Gymnasium,* the brothers had received a solid foundation in the classics, but little exposure to the social and physical sciences. Neither there nor at Eden did the program lead to a bachelor's degree. In 1914 Reinhold wrote back to Eden from graduate school at Yale, lamenting his lack of a degree. He also complained that his seminary experience had not prepared him to do research in primary sources.[10] For his part, Richard urged the synod to conform its system of higher education to American standards. In his senior year at Eden, he used his position as editor of *The Keryx* to call for a new curriculum at Elmhurst, one that

---

[7]HRN, "Winter Peace," *Keryx* 2 (December 1912): 1.

[8]HRN, "Youth," *Keryx* 4 (June 1914): 1.

[9]Th. C. Seybold, "Criticism on 'Paper on Shelley' by Mr. H. Niebuhr," Papers of the "Lincoln Lyceum," 1909-1918, Eden Theological Seminary Archives, Webster Groves MO (italics added).

[10]Reinhold Niebuhr, "Yale-Eden," *Keryx* 4 (December 1914): 1-4.

included not only an A.B. degree, but an expanded faculty and library, stiffer entrance requirements, and instruction in English.[11]

Such measures threatened those dedicated to the status quo. Yet the wheel of change was beginning to turn in Niebuhr's favor. As America moved toward a declaration of war against Germany, leaders of the Evangelical Synod seemed more willing to listen to the new generation. One of these was Dr. Samuel D. Press, the first native-born American to hold a faculty post at Eden and the first full-time professor to teach his classes in English instead of German. Press had studied theology in Germany under Adolf von Harnack and Reinhold Seeburg, but his point of view was American. For both Niebuhrs he soon became the model of a creative scholar and teacher who kept abreast of recent developments in theology. In Reinhold's estimation, Press "proved the point that an educational institution needs only to have Mark Hopkins on one end of a log and a student on the other."[12] The copy of *Social Sources* that Richard gave to Press contained a handwritten inscription describing his old mentor as "the teacher who first and more than any other taught me to love and follow the truth whithersoever it might lead, and to whom as to a second father this volume should also have been dedicated."[13]

2

An examination of the years between the outset of the war, when he was still a student at Eden, and 1919, when he was appointed to the faculty of that seminary, reveals much about Richard Niebuhr's ambivalent attitude toward the denomination of his forebears. By the time he finished his studies in 1915 at Eden, he had become reluctant simply to serve as another "German minister" in the Evangelical pattern. As president of his graduating class, he wrote the customary "Farewell" to his Alma Mater in German, but depicted himself and his classmates as stepping over the threshold of an uncertain future.[14] Richard's real hope seems to have been to go on to Yale, as Gustav Niebuhr had encouraged Reinhold to do before him. Instead, financial constraints brought on by his father's death forced Richard to return home to accept a job from his eldest brother Walter on the Lincoln, Illinois, newspaper. Not until

---

[11]HRN, "Our Educational System," *Keryx* 5 (February 1915): 16-17.

[12]See Reinhold Niebuhr, "Intellectual Autobiography," in *Reinhold Niebuhr: His Religious, Social, and Political Thought,* ed. Charles W. Kegley and Robert W. Bretall (New York, 1956) 3-4.

[13]This copy of *Social Sources* is in the possession of Press's son, Walter, now living in California. For an analysis of Press and his influence on the Niebuhr brothers, see William G. Chrystal, "Samuel D. Press: Teacher of the Niebuhrs," *Church History* 53 (December 1984): 504-21.

[14]For his "Farewell," see HRN, "Vale," *Keryx* 5 (June 1915): 2.

a year later did he choose to be ordained and to become pastor of the Walnut Park Evangelical Church. But no sooner had he begun his parish duties than he also started work on his first academic degree at Washington University in Saint Louis.

Niebuhr sought to capitalize on his denominational background in order to establish his credentials in the new environment. At Washington University his major was German and his thesis topic a critical study of a German poet. Entitled "The Problem of the Individual in Richard Dehmel," the thesis dealt with Dehmel's battle to break out of the fetters of his environment, which paralleled Niebuhr's battle against parochialism in his church. To free his soul from its external molding, the German poet at first indulged himself in selfishness. But he soon realized that the individual who made a god out of self was asserting neither freedom nor the higher values he sought, but obeying simply "the demands of an animal." The poet felt himself a true individual only after he was able to transcend the finite realm and identify himself with the "World Soul." For Dehmel, creative art was the best path to self-transcendence. Poetry involved him in a purpose that encompassed the whole of life and nature. While it retained a distinctively individual stamp, it also contributed to the well-being of others.[15] The same struggle was to appear in the background of the analysis Niebuhr later made of Christian denominations in America. For him, an outwardly divided Christianity became a "religious failure" because it chained the ideals of Christ to the values of human cultures. This fettering process he perceived to be part of denominationalism's "social sources."

Prior to completing his Ph.D. at Yale in 1924, Niebuhr enrolled in no less than six different graduate level programs at various American universities.[16] At Washington, the combination of courses in psychology and philosophy for his minor helped fill some of the holes in his undergraduate education. He also enjoyed such instructors as Charles Edward Cory, an expert on Hegel who was educated at Yale and Harvard and who studied the spiritual interests of humankind from a purely secular point of view. But for the spring term in 1919 Niebuhr moved on to New York City and enrolled at both Columbia University and Union Theological Seminary. While there he touched almost every important base in the curriculum of one of liberalism's prestigious strongholds. He studied church history with A. C. McGiffert, philosophy of religion with Eugene Lyman, Christian ethics with Harry Ward, and practical theology with

---

[15]HRN, "The Problem of the Individual in Richard Dehmel" (M.A. thesis, Washington University, 1917).

[16]The list includes Washington University in St. Louis, Columbia University, Union Theological Seminary in New York, the University of Michigan, the University of Chicago, and Yale University.

Harry Emerson Fosdick.[17] Later that same year, Samuel D. Press, by then president of Eden, appointed Niebuhr to the seminary faculty. Yet even after he returned to Saint Louis to assume this new position, he continued to commute back and forth to Washington University in order to participate in graduate seminars in sociology led in the fall and spring terms of 1919-1920 by George Ware Stephens, a professor interested in the economic aspects of American culture, and in 1921-1922 by Walter Bodenhafer, a young sociologist trained at the University of Chicago.[18] Also while teaching at Eden, he spent the summers broadening his competence in psychology and sociology—in 1920 at the University of Michigan and in 1922 at the University of Chicago. "Academic vagabondage" was the name Reinhold Niebuhr gave to all of this advanced study.[19] However, it clearly stemmed from Richard's deep desire to achieve both scholarly competence and a view of things that was broader than the one his Evangelical Synod had offered him.

World War I broke out while Niebuhr was still a student at Eden Seminary. As editor of *The Keryx* he carefully refrained from specifying what role America ought to play in the conflict, but he did not deny the sympathy for Germany that he and other Eden students felt because of their ancestry and the influence of German scholarship upon their education. After the sinking of the *Lusitania* in 1915, however, it became increasingly unpopular to take this position. When Niebuhr's predecessor at Walnut Park openly supported Germany's war aims, for instance, he was censured by neighborhood authorities. Niebuhr, on the other hand, saw the war as an opportunity to institute sweeping change in the life of this typical congregation of the Evangelical Synod. Shortly after his arrival as the new minister in 1916, he began by expressing concern that the young people could not understand the German spoken in sermons and confirmation classes, and within a year started conducting the congregation's first worship services in English. The step aroused the opposition of Walnut Park's older generation, many of whom feared that the change in language would destroy the beauty and meaning of their heritage. But Nie-

---

[17]Information made available by James A. Hayes, registrar of Union Theological Seminary, in letter to author, 1 May 1981.

[18]Information about the courses Niebuhr took at Washington University and the professors who taught them made available by William Priest, assistant to the archivist at Washington University, St. Louis, in letter to author, 1 June 1981.

[19]Reinhold Niebuhr, "On Academic Vagabondage," first published in *Keryx* in 1924; reprinted in *Young Reinhold Niebuhr: His Early Writings*, ed. William G. Chrystal (St. Louis, 1977) 145-50.

buhr persisted in using English in the performance of most of his parish duties.[20]

When America entered the war in 1917, Niebuhr immediately gave his wholehearted support to the Allied cause and joined other members of his family in working for the War Welfare Commission of the Evangelical Synod. Created for the purpose of helping Evangelical service personnel away from home, the commission turned into a Niebuhr family operation. Reinhold was appointed executive secretary. To enable the elder brother to remain at Bethel Church in Detroit, their mother Lydia took up his parish duties during the week. Sister Hulda assisted with the stenographer's chores. Richard helped handle commission business and correspondence in Saint Louis. He also wrote "Fling Out the Banner," a hymn intended for distribution to soldiers in the field. The lyrics reflect a staunchly pro-American stance, concluding in the final stanza,

Fling out, fling out the banner,
In lands across the sea,
Where our brave lads are battling:
They battle Lord, for Thee!
Oh, have them in Thy keeping
In lands beyond the sea;
And if we lay them sleeping,
We trust their souls to Thee.[21]

Niebuhr took the additional step of enlisting as an army chaplain. He was ordered to report to camp for schooling in the summer of 1918, but the war ended before he was able to serve any troops in the field.[22]

3

The course of Richard Niebuhr's career during the decade following World War I served to intensify his feelings related to his sense of ethnic identity. By 1920 his life seemed ripe with new possibilities. He was married during the

---

[20]Albert Hoetker, Lillian Schaefer, and Henrietta Swanson (three members of Walnut Park Evangelical Church during Niebuhr's ministry there), interview with author, St. Louis MO, 1 March 1972.

[21]HRN, "Fling Out the Banner," 1917, in a printed pamphlet published by the Board of Sunday Schools of the Evangelical Synod, H. Richard Niebuhr Papers, Eden Theological Seminary Archives. See also William G. Chrystal, "Reinhold Niebuhr and the First World War," *Journal of Presbyterian History* 55 (Fall 1977): 386-98.

[22]John Baltzer, president of the Evangelical Synod, to Reinhold Niebuhr (mistakenly addressed as Rev. H. Niebuhr), 2 July 1918, Eden Theological Seminary Archives. In the letter Baltzer said, "I am glad to learn that Rev. H. Niebuhr and Rev. D. Balzer have received notice to report to Camp Taylor at the Chaplains School." See also "Report of the Secretary," War Welfare Commission, Detroit, Michigan, 26 June 1918, Eden Theological Seminary Archives. Here Rev. H. Niebuhr is listed as a chaplaincy candidate.

summer of that year to Florence Marie Mittendorf, whom he had first met in his father's congregation in Lincoln, Illinois. Their household soon came to include two children, Cynthia and Richard Reinhold.

Meanwhile, the hysteria and superpatriotism of "100 percent Americans" had accelerated the Evangelical Synod's shift away from the use of the German language. At Eden Seminary Niebuhr was in fact presenting all of his New Testament and sociology lectures in English. Yet, in his estimation, this change made the denomination's deficiencies all the more glaring. At Elmhurst College in particular, requirements for admission still included Evangelical church membership and a pastor's recommendation. The lack of accreditation, restrictive curriculum, stress on piety over scholarship, student enrollment of less than two hundred, and chronic shortages of funds continued to limit its potential.

As president of Elmhurst from 1924 to 1927 Niebuhr wasted no time in moving to revitalize the college. His first step was to launch a "Four Year Plan" intended to bring full accreditation by 1929. This involved the collection of a $400,000 endowment, appropriations for the improvement and expansion of campus facilities, and the reorganization of the faculty into eight departments, each headed by a person holding a Ph.D. Subsequently, Niebuhr initiated a series of reforms designed to bring Elmhurst's faculty and curriculum into conformity with the accepted American standards for higher education. For the first time in its history, the school adopted an academic ranking system, a faculty salary scale, and a program of sabbatical leaves. German language courses no longer received top priority. In Niebuhr's view, they had become a burden on students who were incapable of becoming "bi-lingual preachers." What students really needed to develop, he thought, was their facility for broad reading, independent thinking, and research.

Elmhurst, he also argued, should open its doors to women students and to young people from other communions in order to boost enrollment and balance its budget. This would require a broadened curriculum, aimed at those who were interested in careers other than the ministry.[23] The result, he told his critics, would actually enrich the education of the institution's pretheological students, not corrupt them. They would be "challenged" to make a "clear-cut decision" for the ministry, not "drift" into it.[24] Once it had acquired this greater internal diversity, Niebuhr argued, the college would have stronger re-

---

[23]HRN to Dr. Samuel D. Press, 8 January 1925; HRN to Miss E. L. Ebert, 21 July 1926; "General Letter to the Brethren of the Evangelical Synod," 30 September 1925, HRN Papers, Elmhurst College Archives, Elmhurst IL.

[24]HRN Memorandum, "Proseminary or College?" n.d., HRN Papers, Elmhurst College Archives.

lationships with the surrounding community. These Niebuhr sought to promote by establishing a School of Music, providing evening classes in religion for the townspeople, opening the library to the public, and making scholarships available to graduates of the local high school.[25]

Eventually Niebuhr set forth his hopes in two imaginative visions. One was an idealistic "Ten Year Plan" that came to include a Chicago architect's sketch of a colonial-style campus, peopled by six hundred students, and built around an open mall of sunken gardens and pools leading up to a chapel with an imposing spire. The other was a plan to merge the Protestant colleges of DuPage County, namely Elmhurst, Wheaton, and Northwestern Colleges, into a new "Dupage University." Such a federation, Niebuhr argued, would reduce the number of tiny schools produced by denominational pride and enable them to pool their resources and ideas so as to develop special programs and attract first-rate faculties.[26]

In an ethnically bound denomination such as the Evangelical Synod, these achievements seem truly remarkable. But the demands of the presidency at Elmhurst soon exhausted Niebuhr. In each of his first two years he pushed himself to the edge of a nervous breakdown. Especially frustrating were some of the administrative realities. The synod, for instance, retained the right to reduce its direct subsidy to Elmhurst, yet it refused to give the college board the authority to borrow money to meet current expenditures. This forced the president constantly to solicit donations from individual congregations and their auxiliary groups. A full teaching load and numerous committee responsibilities in the synod also deprived Niebuhr of any time for his first love—theological study. So in 1927 he decided to leave Elmhurst and to return to teaching at Eden Seminary.[27]

In *Social Sources* Niebuhr approached the recent history of immigrant churches much as he did his own denomination's Americanization. He outlined developments that required further study if the process of assimilation were to be fully understood. As he saw it, immigrant denominations were caught in the conflicting processes of "accommodation" and "differentiation." In the nineteenth century, for example, variations in the degree of accommodation had contributed to a division of the Dutch Reformed churches. When the old

---

[25]William F. Denman, "Elmhurst: Development Study of a Church-Related College" (Ph.D. diss., Syracuse University, 1966) 196-97. Denman notes that more than seventy-five people from the community took advantage of music and religion classes in 1926.

[26]HRN, "Memorandum—Subject: Dupage University," 28 November 1925, HRN Papers, Elmhurst College Archives.

[27]HRN to Rev. D. Bruning, chairman of the General Board of Educational Institutions of the Evangelical Synod, 7 January 1927, HRN Papers, Elmhurst College Archives.

Reformed Church in America gave up the ancient practice of singing psalms and started using American hymns, the True Dutch Reformed Church, composed largely of immigrant congregations, was organized to conserve the older creeds and customs. Similar differences in rates of assimilation kept Lutherans of the Missouri Synod apart from the older Lutheran communities in the General Synod; and they contributed to the atomization of the Scandinavian Lutherans into a score of Norwegian, Swedish, and Danish denominations. Niebuhr predicted that once immigration trailed off and the "melting pot" had done its job, immigrant churches of the same general background would be drawn into union.[28]

The book also pinpointed a source of controversy in the immigrant churches with which Niebuhr's experience in the Evangelical Synod had made him familiar, namely, the language question. The adoption of English as the church language, he stressed, was a difficult but inevitable aspect of the longer process of adjustment to American culture. When it appeared to threaten the ethnic identities of particular congregations, it led to controversies that tended to weaken their chances of survival in a competitive religious environment. In eighteenth-century New York, for instance, the Dutch Reformed congregations were convulsed over the introduction of English; pastors attempted to maintain the Dutch language in order to keep their members dissociated from the newly arrived Scotch-Irish Calvinists whom they considered uncultured. After the American Revolution, when a younger generation of German Lutherans came into conflict with their parents over the retention of the old language, the various synods divided into "German" and "English" congregations. And early in the nineteenth century, the German Reformed churches in Pennsylvania moved toward cooperation with German Lutherans, not because of increasing doctrinal agreement but because the "Anglicization" of their denominations had undermined the old linguistic source of solidarity. The hypothesis Niebuhr set forth was that when the process of accommodation to American culture muted the language question, immigrant denominations tended to maintain their competitive edge by placing new emphasis on distinctive doctrines. "Ecclesiastical and doctrinal issues replace the cultural lines of division, and loyalty of an English-speaking, second generation is fostered by appeal to different motives than were found effective among immigrants themselves," he wrote. "Denominational separateness in a competitive situation finds its justification under these circumstances in the accentuation of theological or liturgical peculiarities of the group."[29]

---

[28]HRN, *Social Sources of Denominationalism,* 214-20.

[29]Ibid., 229.

4

Who is the better analyst of anyone's religious life? The "insider" who has lived the behavior he or she describes? Or the more detached "outsider?" In Niebuhr's case, the isolationism and cultural parochialism he perceived in his own Evangelical Synod appear to have prejudiced his view of immigrant churches in America. In *Social Sources* he gave a negative evaluation of religion's function among all such tightly knit groups. Their institutions, as he saw them, were anachronistic, serving to reinforce national and racial attitudes that were essentially sectarian. Historians since Niebuhr have demonstrated that the intertwining of ethnicity and religion is far more complex than he suggested. Some have even argued the contrary that emigration to America reinforced a process of adaptation to the modern world that had already begun in Europe. Certainly for many new arrivals, the immigrant congregations provided a faith that was oriented to the future and encouraged not only education but economic advancement and upward social mobility.[30]

For his own immigrant church, Richard Niebuhr's goal was assimilation. But was this process sufficient to enlarge the Evangelical Synod's influence on American life? As Niebuhr saw it, something else was necessary. As early as 1922, in "A Sociological Interpretation of Eden," he urged the synod to reevaluate its outlook on the church's role in the world. This little-known article outlined the direction he wanted not only the seminary but the entire synod to go. The value of a community to its individual members seemed to increase, he wrote, when its interests became more "universal." It must do more than combat friction from within; it must build relationships with other communities and join forces with those that share its larger concerns. For a community like Eden, this implied a "sympathy with all the aspirations of men toward God and His kingdom,—whether those aspirations be expressed in the language of religion or of economics, whether in the language of the Catholic or of the Protestant, of the American or the German." Only in this way, he believed, could either Eden Seminary or the Evangelical Synod fit into the larger movement of human culture toward the kingdom of God.[31]

Niebuhr tried especially to encourage the synod to become more sympathetic with the labor movement. Among most Christians at the time, the issue

---

[30]See Timothy L. Smith, "New Approaches to the Study of Immigration in Twentieth-Century America," *American Historical Review* 71 (1965-1966): 1265-79; idem, "Lay Initiative in the Life of American Immigrants, 1880-1950," in *Anonymous Americans: Explorations in Nineteenth-Century Social History,* ed. Tamara K. Hareven (Englewood Cliffs NJ, 1971) 214-49; idem, "Religion and Ethnicity in America," *American Historical Review* 83 (December 1978): 1155-85. See also the essays of Josef Barton, William Calush, and Robert Mirak in *Immigrants and Religion in Urban America,* ed. Randall Miller and Thomas Marzik (Philadelphia, 1977).

[31]HRN, "A Sociological Interpretation of Eden," *Keryx* 12 (February 1922): 8-11.

of labor's use of coercive force, sometimes leading to violence, was keeping the church at a distance. But for him, there was obvious hypocrisy involved in preaching "peace" to labor while condoning acts of violence on the part of labor's enemies. Self-preservation seemed to provide the motive. Christians, in his view, were overlooking the implicitly "religious" characteristics of the labor movement. The workers' dissent from the status quo represented a type of "repentance" that helped to make for a better world. It also tended to reinforce the type of "respect for individuality" that Christians gave to children, to women, to the poor and outcast. Perhaps the labor movement did not share the church's loyalty to Christ, but it displayed a loyalty to humanity, a sense of belonging to others, and a capacity for self-sacrifice that were almost "Christian" in character.[32] In Niebuhr's estimation, the church and labor were natural allies in a society in which "rugged individualism" had become rampant and the profit motive was undercutting human values. So he called on his denomination to support the right of workers to organize, to recognize their rights to share in the control of industry, and to endorse reduction of the work day and increases in wages.[33]

In this regard Niebuhr seemed at home with the ethical idealism undergirding the social gospel movement. Very much in the spirit of Walter Rauschenbusch, he viewed the kingdom of God as a social entity embracing all of human life, a community in which relationships were governed by the precepts of love and brotherhood. Like Rauschenbusch, he was not anticapitalist. Nor did he believe that industrialization was inherently evil. He simply condemned the greed and inhumanity connected with it. The difficulty, as he saw it, was that these vices had become ingrained in the structures of Western society. But the remedy remained religious, and the primary task of the church was to proclaim the higher righteousness Jesus set forth in the Sermon on the Mount, to develop communities in which that righteousness could come to group expression, and to use all the resources available to give preference to human values over economic ones.

At Elmhurst Niebuhr proposed several programs designed to give students at Elmhurst an understanding of the social impact of their faith and its application to the problems of modern society. Speakers like Paul Hutchinson, managing editor of *Christian Century,* were invited to give the commencement address. Clubs were encouraged to explore national and international issues.

---

[32]HRN, "The Alliance Between Labor and Religion," *Theological Magazine of the Evangelical Synod of North America* 49 (May 1921): 197-203. For related material, see HRN, "Bible Teachings About Work," *Evangelical Home* 1 (Spring 1921): 85-88.

[33]HRN, "Christianity and the Social Problem," *Theological Magazine of the Evangelical Synod of North America* 50 (July 1922): 278-91.

The college's board of trustees was asked to consider recruiting students and new faculty from black and other minorities as a way of helping to break down racial barriers. As Niebuhr himself put it,

> I trust that the time will come when we can make a practical experiment in practical Christianity through the breaking down of racial barriers in our midst by introducing not only into our student body but also into our faculty members of other races than the much praised Nordic tribes. Certainly such a step might accomplish much to teach all of us in our community to meet the members of other races with respect, admiration and understanding.[34]

New courses on the application of Christian ethics to banking practices and labor problems were also proposed. "The graduation of an occasional student who would achieve leadership in the application of Christianity to business or industry," Niebuhr wrote in his annual report to the board, "would be as important a contribution to humanity as the graduation of a brilliant theological student."[35] Clearly in line with these proposals was the Elmhurst Service Conference of 1927. A three-day affair regarded by Niebuhr as "the greatest single event in Elmhurst history," the conference featured representatives from several professions presenting problems that challenged the Christian conscience. Reinhold Niebuhr, for example, discussed what he considered to be the evils of industrialism in the light of the gospel of Jesus. Others focused on the challenges posed by racial animosity, the psychological effects of modern industry, and the role of Western imperialism in the history of China.[36]

Such sympathies called forth adjustments in the theology of the Evangelical Synod. In the nineteenth century its leaders had expressed the social element in their piety by establishing hospitals, charities, and asylums. Gustav Niebuhr had helped establish a home for epileptics in Saint Charles, Missouri. During America's Progressive era, the synod's leaders had allied their organization with the movement for social Christianity sufficiently enough to take it into the Federal Council of Churches, and such persons as Washington Gladden and Walter Rauschenbusch had appeared as lecturers at Eden Seminary. But the leaders had made no commitment to reconstructing the social order. Richard Niebuhr's remedy for this deficiency was to shift the synod's allegiance from the Lutheran to the Calvinist side of its theological heritage. In Calvin he found a more prophetic vision of the kingdom of God, one that sought

---

[34]HRN, "Report to the Board of Trustees of Elmhurst College," 31 January 1927, p. 9, HRN Papers, Elmhurst College Archives.

[35]Ibid., 10.

[36]"The Elmhurst Service Conference," *Evangelical Herald* 26 (21 April 1927): 327, and ibid. (28 April 1927): 344-45.

to bring the affairs of society under the rule of Christ. "Whether Jesus conceived that the Kingdom was to be established here or beyond is a question beside the point," Niebuhr wrote already in 1921. "The righteousness of the gospel" remained "the righteousness of community conduct."[37] There is no doubt that Niebuhr wanted active involvement in his denomination to imply an active commitment to social Christianity. In the twenties this translated into support for the outlawry of war, the Federal Council's "Social Ideals for the Churches," a child-labor amendment to the Constitution, and the thorough application of Christian teachings to business, industry, politics, race relations, and international affairs.[38]

Richard and Reinhold Niebuhr were in fundamental agreement on this issue. Many of their fellow members of the Evangelical Synod still considered themselves more Lutheran than Reformed in orientation. Some even looked for an eventual merger of the synod with one of the Lutheran denominations. But the Niebuhr brothers found Martin Luther's approach to society too quietistic, too narrowly focused on the salvation of individual souls, and therefore incapable of mating the Christian faith with social ethics. To their way of thinking, the Calvinists, including the Puritans in America, had tended to lapse into legalism by confounding their own moral rules with eternal truth. Yet they had not failed, as Lutherans had, to promote the regeneration of society, which the higher righteousness of the Sermon on the Mount demanded of Christians in every age. Any union with a Lutheran group, Reinhold warned, would result in a surrendering of this emphasis. It could only force the Evangelicals to conform to a limited social outlook.[39]

But how could a single denomination hope to bring such a set of social commitments to bear on a culture as large as America's? Richard Niebuhr was convinced that Christians must first purge their own houses of the divisiveness for which they sought to condemn the world. Only then would they possess the strength needed to exert a strong influence on society. For his own Evangelical Synod, he prescribed a renewal of its earlier interest in merging with other denominations. Stimulated in 1925 by the return of synodical represen-

---

[37]HRN, "Christianity and the Social Problem," 279.

[38]Commission on Christianity and Social Problems, Rev. J. H. Horstmann, chairman, *Official Reports and District Resolutions to the General Conference of the Evangelical Synod of North America, St. Louis, Missouri, 1925* (n.p., n.d.) 224-29; see also idem, *Reports and Minutes of the Twenty-Fifth General Conference of the Evangelical Synod of North America, Rochester, New York, 8-15 October 1929* (n.p., n.d.).

[39]Reinhold Niebuhr, "Where Shall We Go?" an article originally published in the March 1919 issue of *Magazin für Evangelische Theologie und Kirche*, in *Young Reinhold Niebuhr*, 101-108.

tatives to the first ecumenical conference on Life and Work in Stockholm and his association with like-minded Evangelical clergy in Chicago, Niebuhr became an enthusiastic supporter of what he called "the biggest pipe dream we could dream," a plan for uniting the synod with the Reformed church and the United Brethren.[40]

On his return to the Eden faculty in 1927, he immediately accepted an appointment to his denomination's Committee on Relations with Other Churches and became its chairperson. He quickly assumed leadership in joint meetings, working to construct a platform on which the three churches might stand together. When this platform had been hammered out in 1929 as the Plan of Union, Niebuhr supported it. He urged its immediate ratification by the Evangelical Synod and sought patiently to allay the misgivings of conferences and pastors toward it. The United Brethren, however, found little support for the plan among the rank and file. Less democratic in their polity and more stringent in their piety than the Evangelicals or the Reformed, they shortly put an end to the hope of a "United Church in America" by withdrawing from the discussions. The reasons why the United Brethren withdrew from the Plan of Union are not entirely clear. Louis W. Goebel thought that a passage in the United Brethren's *Book of Discipline* forbidding ministers to smoke became an issue that was blown out of proportion. Niebuhr seems to have thought that the United Brethren would find it difficult to give up their episcopal form of polity.[41]

For Niebuhr, the frustrated enterprise furnished a valuable set of lessons. During the course of the negotiations he came to recognize that idealistic rhetoric must be tempered with an awareness of practical difficulties. Union had the greatest chance of success where there were only minor differences in church polity, social attitudes, and cultural heritage.[42] The problem of Christian disunity, as he now saw it, lay not simply with denominational structures, but with the fractures in the culture in which they resided. As assimilation progressed and the culture became more homogeneous, denominational mergers became more feasible. Still, this process was as likely to accentuate old divisions, or even to produce new ones, as it was to bring about greater unity. Niebuhr had first expressed this fear in 1924, as he was beginning to recognize that the process of entering the mainstream of American life might diminish as well as

---

[40]HRN to Louis W. Goebel, 2 November 1926, HRN Papers, Eden Theological Seminary Archives.

[41]See Goebel, *Recollections,* 90; also HRN to Rev. John Baltzer, 18 June 1928, HRN Papers, Eden Theological Seminary Archives.

[42]See HRN, "Churches That Might Unite," *Christian Century* 46 (21 February 1929): 259-61.

enhance his Evangelical Synod's influence in the world. "As we leave the sectarianism of race behind," he told the denomination's membership, "we need to be on our guard lest a worse sectarianism, that of economic class, overtake us." Niebuhr's concern was that as the farmers and small businessmen who made up the bulk of the Evangelical Synod prospered, it might become "just another middle-class church."[43] Apparent to him in 1929 was the fact that all of organized Christianity might even become redivided into a series of national churches, each projecting the political and cultural interests of its own people rather than an international form of faith.[44]

Thus, even as he completed *Social Sources,* Niebuhr's interest in overcoming the problem of Christian disunity at the organizational level seems to have been on the wane. In the final chapter, he issued a prophetic call for a noninstitutional form of the church, a "universal fellowship" committed to the Christian ideals of love and brotherhood.[45] Following the collapse of the plan for a United Church in America, the Evangelical Synod continued discussions with the Reformed church and in 1934 entered into union with it. But Niebuhr assumed no leadership role in the process after 1930.

5

Paradoxically, the strength of Niebuhr's firsthand experience again became the greatest weakness of another position he took in *Social Sources.* Given the commitment he made to the cause of ecumenism in his own denomination, he did not see, as Winthrop Hudson and Sidney Mead did in the 1950s, that denominations in America might be members of a family of religious bodies; they differed in their attempts to give visible expression to the life of the church, but each body was the heir of a common faith and shared the common aim to bring the Christian influence to bear on the life of the world. Nor could Niebuhr offer the perspective that Elwyn Smith and Timothy Smith did in the 1960s, the view that denominations were born of "social necessity," as a way of giving guidance, support, and discipline to widely scattered congregations and providing an administrative structure that would expedite spreading of the gospel, help keep the nation morally sound, and resist public infidelity. Nor was Niebuhr in any position, as Andrew Greeley and Martin Marty were in the 1970s, to suggest that denominational Christianity reflected the vitality and vigor of a pluralistic society, providing a way for ethnic groups to find meaning

---

[43]HRN, "The Kingdom, Our Country and Our Church," *Evangelical Herald* 24 (19 November 1924): 760.

[44]HRN, "Churches That Might Unite," 259-61.

[45]HRN, *Social Sources of Denominationalism,* 278-84.

and identity.[46] Instead, Niebuhr used the term *denomination* in an entirely pejorative fashion. He thought of it as a form of religious capitulation to the world, and as a synonym for sectarian exclusivism.

The cutting edge of Niebuhr's thinking, however, remained focused on the theme of church and world. In *Social Sources* he followed Ernst Troeltsch in defining the problem of the world as one of harnessing its plurality of interests, classes, and races and integrating them into a single, harmonious society committed to a common set of objectives. Such a "synthesis of culture" not only was vital to the life of any society, but was a function Christianity always had performed well.[47] In 1937 Niebuhr's volume entitled *The Kingdom of God in America* set forth in its title his synthesizing principle for America's culture. The church's dilemma, as he saw it, was no less acute. To help bring about a cultural synthesis, it could not escape involvement "in the world." But how could the church so involved preserve its integrity and not become "of the world?"

During his early years in the Evangelical Synod, Niebuhr clearly recognized this side of the problem, too. In fact, he asserted that the church must maintain a constant rhythm of "identification" with culture and "withdrawal" from it. While it must accommodate itself to a complex and changing world, lest it lose its effectiveness, the church must also remember that "accommodation" again and again has led to a "radical denial of the universalism or righteousness of the gospel." For this reason, there must be periods of "withdrawal" for the church to regain a sense of its own peculiar identity and to prepare itself for another plunge into the world.[48]

Along with other church leaders at the time, Niebuhr was obviously perplexed by Protestantism's weakened influence in American life. For almost a century prior to World War I, its old-line churches had marched together in what church historian Robert Handy has called "the quest for a Christian America." Though their responses to new intellectual trends had varied, they had joined in a common effort to "Christianize" the nation. In spite of crucial differences in philosophies governing the application of social action techniques, this fundamental unity of Protestants was not seriously affected. For Sidney Mead, the "wonder" was not that the massive challenges of the nineteenth century had produced "a great deal of confusion, inanity, and hysteria but that as much sanity and order prevailed . . . as actually did." Yet this growth and unity had masked a retreat from theological issues and a compromising of religious integrity. In the often quoted words of Henry Steele Commager,

---

[46]For an excellent collection of literature on the subject, see Russell E. Richey, ed., *Denominationalism* (Nashville, 1977).

[47]HRN, *Social Sources of Denominationalism,* 267-68.

[48]HRN, "The Church in the Modern World," *Keryx* 20 (May 1929): 9-10, 29.

"[Organized] religion prospered while theology went slowly bankrupt." And as described by Winthrop Hudson, it was largely the "story of the Halfway Covenant" all over again. "Long before the advent of the automobile, the motion picture, the radio and Sunday golf, disintegration had set in," he notes. "Discipline declined, evangelistic fervor faded, faith lost its force, and the churches living at peace with the world, lost their sense of a distinct and specific vocation in society."[49] So when Protestantism's zeal for bringing the moral claims of Christianity to bear on the nation began to flag, the divisions and weaknesses that success had previously obscured became more apparent.

"Religious depression" is the term most often used to describe the mounting indifference and hostility toward religion in the postwar climate of the 1920s. Fundamentalists and a wide spectrum of other evangelical Protestants, to be sure, were flourishing.[50] Yet in the major old-line denominations, missionary fervor, funds, and church and Sunday School attendance were all on the decline. The social gospel, once so strong, was now retreating in the face of a tendency to look upon the "new business" as the true road to social salvation. Torn by internal conflicts, the churches seemed unable to agree on anything except the socially divisive issues of Prohibition and anti-Catholicism.[51] As H. L. Mencken wrote in 1925, "That Protestantism in this great Christian realm is down with a wasting disease must be obvious to every amateur of ghostly pathology. The denominational papers are full of alarming reports from its bedside, and all sorts of projects for the relief of the patient."[52]

In Niebuhr's estimation, the problem had arisen because Protestantism's deep involvement "in" the world had brought economic, political, and racial entanglements that made it too much "of" the world. This he asserted as early as 1925 in the first article he published in the *Christian Century*. Entitled "Back to Benedict," it called on Protestantism's old-line denominations to reaffirm the monastic ideal. The liberal movement of the nineteenth century, as he saw it, had helped these denominations adapt to the modern world. It had awakened among Christians a renewed emphasis on ethical applications of the gos-

---

[49]Robert T. Handy, "The Protestant Quest for a Christian America, 1830-1930," *Church History* 23 (March 1952): 8-20; Sidney E. Mead, *The Lively Experiment: The Shaping of Christianity in America* (New York, 1963) 157; Henry Steele Commager, *The American Mind: An Interpretation of American Thought and Character Since the 1880's* (New Haven, 1950) 165; Winthrop S. Hudson, *The Great Tradition of the American Churches* (New York, 1953) 225.

[50]Joel A. Carpenter, "Fundamentalist Institutions and the Rise of Evangelical Protestantism, 1929-1942," *Church History* 49 (March 1980): 62-75.

[51]Robert T. Handy, "The American Religious Depression, 1925-1935," *Church History* 29 (March 1960): 3-16.

[52]H. L. Mencken, "Editorial," *American Mercury* 4 (March 1925): 286.

pel and had strengthened the hope of reordering society. But at the same time, it had allowed the world to compromise the church. The "holy" God whom the Reformers had rediscovered was obscured by their modern heirs, who in their preoccupation with the discussion of humankind's better aspirations, were now ready to equate God's kingdom with the "progress" of Western culture. The "way out," Niebuhr argued, "may be the way of the monk." Only by withdrawing from the world, he seems to have meant, could Christianity unfetter itself enough to recover its integrity. Traditionally, to be sure, Protestants had found such measures repugnant. Yet the simplicity and hardness of the monastic ideal had helped to purge the church of its materialistic preoccupations and to renew its devotion to the spiritual realm. As some of the "sects" had done in the post-Reformation era, the mission of Christians in the churches of the twentieth century was to reassert the radical demands that Christ's gospel made on a fallen world.[53]

6

Some of the more instructive insights Niebuhr brought to bear on the unedifying Protestant scene of the 1920s came from the work of Troeltsch. The link between his own intellectual patterns and those of this great Berlin professor had been forged with the doctoral dissertation he submitted at Yale in 1924. Well versed in the German language and theology, Niebuhr saw as his chief purpose the completion of the task death had prevented Troeltsch from achieving, namely, a systematic presentation of his own "philosophy of religion." Much later in his career, Niebuhr freely acknowledged the impetus that Troeltsch had given to his thinking. As he observed in the preface to *Christ and Culture,* "I am most conscious of my debt to that theologian and historian who was occupied throughout his life by the problem of church and culture—Ernst Troeltsch. The present book in one sense undertakes to do no more than to supplement and in part correct his work on *The Social Teachings of the Christian Churches.*"[54]

Troeltsch's sociology especially served to deepen Niebuhr's appreciation of the worldly aspects of Christianity. From this perspective, he claimed in 1926, the "orthodox" view that attributed denominational divisions to differences over points of doctrine and practice had led to false analysis. To simply regard Roman Catholics as upholders of a semi-Pelagian view of sin and grace or to intimate that Methodists were Calvinists who had tempered their faith with

---

[53]HRN, "Back to Benedict?" *Christian Century* 42 (2 July 1925): 860-61.

[54]HRN, *Christ and Culture* (New York, 1951) xi-xii.

Arminian modifications obscured the more fundamental economic and social reasons for their differences.[55]

Even more attractive to Niebuhr were the categories of "church" and "sect" which Troeltsch had first applied to the European religious scene. The "church," the more institutional of the two types of religious groups, emphasized a system of doctrine, sacramental rites, education of youth, and the prerogatives of an official clergy. Church membership tended to be "inclusive," coinciding with one's own birth into a family or nation and reflecting the attitudes of society's respectable majority. As the more associational group, a "sect," on the other hand, focused on the religious experience of the individual and relied more on laypersons for leadership. Since it tended to view itself as a heroic minority in an alien society, a "sect" set down more stringent requirements for membership, and in fear that these might be compromised, preferred to isolate itself from the surrounding culture. In marked contrast to the "church," members of a "sect" were drawn from society's outcasts, the poor, and the disenfranchised. In their polity, they also tended to be more democratic than hierarchical. Less important for Niebuhr was "mysticism," a third type of religious grouping in which Troeltsch perceived a tendency to internalize the content of rituals and doctrines and thus transform them into a personal possession of the heart.

Niebuhr's intention was not to label particular denominations as "church" or "sect." Rather, he found the categories helpful in explaining the proliferation of churches in America. Injecting the terms into the ongoing discussion of religion on the frontier, his chapter in *Social Sources* suggested that the frontier environment had helped fashion an emotional religion characterized by revivalistic enthusiasm, lay preaching, and voluntaristic organizations. Only in their ethics of individual morality did persons on the frontier stand apart from Europe's "disinherited." As he saw it, a distinguishing feature of Methodist and Baptist denominations was their success in adapting to the frontier.[56] In his interpretation of the tumultuous period prior to the Civil War, moreover, Niebuhr took note of the differences in the behavior of various groups. Like the sects of the Old World, he argued, the Methodists and Baptists had remained more sensitive to social injustice and inequality. Consequently, when their Southern preachers began to accommodate to the interests of slaveholders, the schism of both was inevitable. The behavior of the Lutherans and Episcopalians, on the other hand, was more in keeping with that of groups with a "church" background. They tended to view the state as divinely ordained and to restrict

---

[55]See HRN, "What Holds Churches Together?" *Christian Century* 43 (18 March 1926): 346-48.

[56]HRN, *Social Sources of Denominationalism,* 140-64.

the application of Christian ethics to the individual and familial phases of human conduct. So their divisions did not come until much later, and when they did, the chief issue was not slavery, but loyalty to the Union.[57]

Of Troeltsch's two religious groups, the "sect" was the type Niebuhr placed in a more favorable light. Established churches in his view had linked themselves with the ruling class and thus had tended since the days of Constantine to subordinate religion to politics. Even in their worship, he felt, such churches had found it difficult to transcend their national consciousness, much less pray for their enemies. Sects, on the other hand, always acting as a counterforce, had shunned politics and taken an uncompromising stand on Christian principles. Unlike church-type groups, they had also refused to believe that war's catastrophes or successes were divinely ordained. Instead, they could and did condemn all wars.[58] In these and other places in *Social Sources,* Niebuhr was holding up sectarian disengagement from the world as a model for the denominations of his day to emulate. Only then, he thought, could they regain their moral integrity.

For Niebuhr, the sociology of the "middle" and the "disinherited" classes shed light on another problem. The older Protestant churches of America were clearly lacking in appeal and influence in working-class circles. Might the failure be attributed to an anti-labor bias? Had the churches ignored the effects of industrialization on society? Was the gospel really an opiate? Niebuhr knew that in the years following the Reformation Calvinism had both facilitated and been shaped by the rise of the bourgeoisie. This was in fact the version of Max Weber's thesis he presented in *Social Sources.*

The connection between Calvinism and the rise of capitalism, as Niebuhr saw it, was a process of "interaction" involving a variety of factors. "In part," he wrote, "it is to be explained by the correspondence existing between principles of the Reformation faith and the religious and moral interests of the bourgeoisie, in part by the ability of Calvinism to produce a middle class through its insistence on those virtues which made the growth of trade and industry and so of the bourgeoisie possible, in part by the success of the economic group in modifying the religion to meet its desires."[59] Niebuhr believed that this modifying influence was clearly apparent in American history. He took the position that middle-class religion neither met the needs of the working classes nor set forth an ethical ideal relevant to their problems.

In such situations in the past, the right leader had preached a religious form of social radicalism based on an uncompromising ethical reading of the gospel.

---

[57]Ibid., 191-99.

[58]Ibid., 106-34.

[59]Ibid., 94.

Such radicalism was fueled by the regenerative theology of conversion. It exalted the religious worth and virtues of the poor, held forth millenarian expectations of their deliverance from social evils, and set new social processes in motion. Niebuhr contended that if the "disinherited" of today were to be brought within the pale of organized Christianity, something similar would have to spark the process.[60]

Though not without some basis, Niebuhr's argument remains open to criticism. Worth noting, for instance, is his caricature of eighteenth-century Methodism in *Social Sources* as the last revolt of the "disinherited," one that forced him, or so it appears, to depict its founders as middle-class betrayers of their own movement and to equate John Wesley's sophisticated theology of sanctification with bourgeois formalism. One of the primary reasons Methodism failed to maintain its influence among the lower economic classes, he argued, was that leaders like Wesley became more interested in correcting individual vices than in reordering society. Furthermore, his idea that socialism in the nineteenth century became a new religious revolt on the part of the "disinherited," substituting the class struggle and the dictatorship of the proletariat for millenarian expectations of the kingdom of God, failed to appreciate fully the difficulties experienced by socialists in marshaling support from the lower economic classes. Niebuhr thus left the erroneous impression that American industrial workers were permanently alienated from all Christian churches.[61]

Social Sources proved to be a pioneering effort to apply the sociological theory of Troeltsch and Weber to the American scene. At work in groups like the Quakers, Niebuhr suggested, was a socioeconomic process that transformed radical religious movements into sects. But with the passing of a generation or two and the rise of many members to the status of middle class, they tended to behave more and more like churches, accommodating themselves rather than resisting the established order. This was Niebuhr's way of explaining class ascendancy in the formation of denominations.[62] The theory is still attractive to sociologists of religion.

At a moral level Niebuhr was portraying the persistence of denominational divisions a a clear sign of the victory of the world over the church. He directed his harshest accusations in *Social Sources* at bourgeois denominations. Their outlook, he explained, was grounded in the notion that riches were the reward for virtue and that poverty was a moral failing not to be pitied but condemned. This gospel of self-help had first tended to take root among Calvinist churches.

---

[60]See HRN, "Christianity and the Industrial Classes," *Theological Magazine of the Evangelical Synod of North America* 57 (June 1929): 12-18.

[61]HRN, *Social Sources of Denominationalism*, 72-76.

[62]Ibid., 39-56.

In time, those who espoused it had succeeded in conquering Calvinism. "A single line of development," he argued, "leads from Jonathan Edwards and his great system of God-centered faith through the Arminianism of the Evangelical revival, the Unitarianism of Channing and Parker, and the humanism of transcendental philosophy, to the man-centered, this-worldly, lift-yourself-by-your-own-bootstraps doctrine of New Thought and Christian Science." In his estimation, the only option left for America's "disinherited" was to find some other home for their faith.[63]

In content as well as tone, then, Richard Niebuhr's sociological analysis of American churches reflected his conflicting feelings about his early experiences in the Evangelical Synod. To that denomination he willingly committed himself as pastor, educator, and leader. Yet in the process of the synod's Americanization following World War I, he chafed under its resistance to assimilation and tasted some of the bittersweet realities that resulted from his efforts to heighten its concern for society and to reclaim the ecumenical aspects of its heritage. This he came to see as a struggle to keep "church" and "world" in their fundamental tension. By the time he wrote *Social Sources,* therefore, he was ready to assert that this same battle was the one all of Christianity in America must fight.

[63]Ibid., 77-105.

H. Richard Niebuhr in the 1930s
(Courtesy Eden Theological Seminary Archives)

CHAPTER II

The Church and the Great Depression

"American Christianity and American culture cannot be understood at all save on the basis of faith in a sovereign, living God."

H. Richard Niebuhr
The Kingdom of God in America, xvi

In 1935 Richard Niebuhr joined forces with two like-minded friends, Wilhelm Pauck and Francis P. Miller, in drafting *The Church Against the World.* Their book contained a major essay by each of the coauthors. Its title, as Niebuhr wrote in his introduction, was not a thesis for debate but the firm declaration of a position. For him and his coauthors, the "salvation" of the church was at stake. Niebuhr claimed that they had witnessed its sometimes brave attempts to promote leagues of nations, pacts outlawing war, associations of international friendship, and organizations of war resisters. But the "march of Mars" continued unabated, and there seemed to be no rebuttal for those hostile critics who had chided the church for siding with the "haves" rather than the "have-nots" of the world. Their theology also informed them that if Christians continued to betray their mission to the oppressed, God would raise another people in their place.[1]

Clearly, the Great Depression was the chief cause of this emergency. By the mid-1930s, its "great knife," as the Lynds put it in their book about their revisit to Middletown, had "cut down impartially through the entire population, cleaving open the lives and hopes of rich as well as poor."[2] No institution

[1]H. Richard Niebuhr (hereafter cited as HRN), "The Question of the Church," in *The Church Against the World,* ed. HRN (Chicago, 1935) 1-6.

[2]Robert L. Lynd and Helen Merrell Lynd, *Middletown in Transition: A Study in Cultural Conflicts* (New York, 1937) 295.

remained unscathed. For the old-line churches in particular, the economic crisis meant slashing budgets, reducing membership, halting benevolent and missionary enterprises, dismissing ministers, closing churches. Beliefs also were in ferment: racial and class antagonisms were sharpened; demagoguery flourished; and victims of the contraction blamed their difficulties variously on politicians, "banksters," welfare loafers, and greedy creditors.[3]

Perplexed church leaders were asking, "Why no revival?" Unlike some economic depressions in the past, this one had triggered no mass movement of the penitent toward the old-line Protestant denominations. Only the newer evangelical and fundamentalist churches, many of them founded during the previous three decades, were experiencing numerical and institutional growth.[4] In liberal organs like the *Christian Century,* the absence of a great "revival" was being explained as a reflection of Protestantism's unqualified alliance with the established order and its failure to develop a corporate definition of evil.[5] Sociologist Samuel C. Kincheloe suggested that the forces that had sparked revivals in the past were now being channeled toward economic solutions to the issues uppermost in the minds of most Americans.[6]

Niebuhr offered a radically different analysis of the problem. In *The Church Against the World* he emphasized modern Christendom's lack of faith in a sovereign God. The real question, he thought, was not how well the church as a whole was measuring up to the expectations of society or functioning as the savior of the civilized world, but how true it was to its divine head. The "cracks of time," he added, had created a golden moment of opportunity for the church to turn away from its temporal relationships toward those that are eternal. So he urged Christians to go to a place of penitence, to retreat into silence and quiet, to return to the Scriptures.[7]

During the Depression years "withdrawal" became a more dominant note in Niebuhr's rhetoric and in the strategy he advocated for the church. Yet at no point did he abandon his earlier commitment to the social gospel. On the contrary, he viewed disengagement from culture as a measure to be undertaken for the sake of that movement's revitalization.

---

[3]See Robert T. Handy, "The American Religious Depression," *Church History* 29 (March 1960): 3-16; and Sydney E. Ahlstrom, *A Religious History of the American People* (New Haven, 1972) 918-21.

[4]Joel A. Carpenter, "Fundamentalist Institutions and the Rise of Evangelical Protestantism, 1929-1942," *Church History* 49 (March 1980): 62-75.

[5]"Why No Revival?" *Christian Century* 52 (18 September 1935): 1169.

[6]Samuel C. Kincheloe, *Research Memorandum on Religion in the Depression* (New York, 1937) 3.

[7]HRN, "The Question of the Church," 12-13.

1

Crucial for interpreting this new phase of Niebuhr's reflections on the theme of church and world are two events in his own life. Both occurred at the outset of the Depression decade. The first was his visit to Europe during a year of sabbatical from Eden Seminary. Early in 1930, with his wife Florence and their children Cynthia and Richard Reinhold, he embarked on the steamer *St. Louis* for a long-awaited period of study and travel. Niebuhr planned to do research in religious philosophy and social ethics at Leipzig, Tübingen, Berlin, and Edinburgh. He also hoped to have enough time to hear Paul Tillich at Frankfurt, Rudolf Bultmann at Marburg, Karl Barth at Bonn, and R. H. Tawney in London. At Tübingen, Niebuhr particularly relished the opportunity to meet Karl Heim. But the encounter turned out to be a disappointment. Niebuhr found that the person whom colleagues touted as "the outstanding theologian of Germany" seemed to be out of touch with Germany's postwar situation.[8]

In Niebuhr's view, the most alarming aspect of that situation was the damage the Treaty of Versailles had done to the morale of the German people. They seemed divided, depressed, and filled with a sense of impending catastrophe. "A favorite word here is 'Schicksal,' " he wrote back home to members of the Evangelical Synod. "It means resignation to the lot of postwar Germany, yet it often seems to imply something nearer despair." "Amerikanismus," he also discovered, was a term Germans used in somewhat the same way Americans used the word "Bolshevism," as a catchall term for everything undesirable. To him the Germans' feelings reflected the heavy burden of reparations payments the Allies had imposed on Germany. These payments, or so the Germans felt, not only kept their own economy depressed, but were padding American pocketbooks by way of French and British banking houses.[9]

All the more obvious to Niebuhr was the appeal of Hitler and his Brownshirts. In spite of his malignant anti-Semitism, Hitler appeared to provide an alternative to the gloom that gripped Germany. His programs offered the hope of recovering the nation's damaged self-respect. His promises to do away with moral filth and civic corruption were attuned completely with middle-class aspirations for an "inner reformation" of their land.[10]

---

[8]HRN to J. H. Horstmann, editor of *Evangelical Herald,* n.d. (marked "received," 26 June 1930); HRN to Horstmann, 29 July 1930, HRN Papers, Eden Theological Seminary Archives, Webster Groves, Missouri.

[9]HRN, "Some Observations on Religious Life in Germany," *Evangelical Herald* 29 (August 1930): 695-96; "German-American Relations," *Evangelical Herald* 29 (4 September 1930): 713, 715.

[10]HRN, "Germany After the Election," *Evangelical Herald* 29 (13 November 1930): 911, 915.

Niebuhr's perceptions of Germany's postwar situation served to balance his perspective on world affairs. Even during World War II he took an especially dim view of church and political leaders who suggested that the cause of one nation was more righteous than another. He saw no circumstances under which an enemy could be branded as evil and thus made to bear the entire load of guilt for war.

Religious life in Germany left a decidedly mixed set of impressions. On his visit to the famous *Kirche zum Heilbronn* in Berlin, Niebuhr entered a packed house of worshipers gathered to hear a popular preacher. The sermon, he felt, was simple, vigorous, and full of conviction. While it lacked depth of insight and freshness of approach, it was still honest and successful in relating the church's beliefs to everyday life. In Leipzig, too, he was impressed by Alfred Dedo Mueller's efforts to conduct open forums with German labor leaders in the hope of reconciling them to the church. Both sides seemed to recognize their need to be more repentant. Leaders urged members of the labor movement not to abandon the church as a relic of the past but to work for its improvement.[11] Clergy like Mueller, however, were too few and far between. Most churches were still trying to live off past traditions. This at least was Niebuhr's reaction to the Lutheran celebration of the four-hundredth anniversary of the Augsburg Confession, which he had made it a point to attend in behalf of the Evangelical Synod. While it was hailed by others as a welcome revival of orthodoxy in Germany, the event for him only seemed to harden the liberal criticisms of older theologians and to add fuel to the fire of Protestant antagonism toward Catholics and socialists.[12]

Confirmation of his doubts came with the subsequent fate of the church in Germany. Soon after Niebuhr's visit ended Hitler seized power and, as he did with other phases of German life, brought the church into line with his fascist program. In the ensuing German "church struggle" Niebuhr openly sympathized with the Confessing Church and such courageous dissenters as Dietrich Bonhoeffer who, unlike the "German Christians," had refused to capitulate to the policies of National Socialism. The church had failed to stop Hitler, Niebuhr wrote in 1933, because it had ignored the patriotism of the German people and neglected to draw the necessary distinctions between national and religious loyalties.[13] Almost three decades later he would use the term "Culture Protestantism" to sum up his reaction to what had occurred in Germany and

---

[11]HRN, "Some Observations on Religious Life in Germany," *Evangelical Herald* 29 (10 July 1930): 556-57; ibid. (17 July 1930): 575.

[12]Ibid. (21 August 1930): 676-77.

[13]HRN, "Nationalism, Socialism and Christianity," *The World Tomorrow* 16 (August 1933): 469-70.

elsewhere during the 1930s. The times, he explained, called for the rejection of this tendency to fuse Christianity with cultural ideologies and for the return of the church to the confession of its "own peculiar faith and ethos."[14]

Far more positive was Niebuhr's assessment of the Soviet Union. During the summer of 1930, while still in Germany, he joined his brother Reinhold and social gospeler Sherwood Eddy on a two-week excursion to Moscow and Leningrad. As for many Americans at the time, the mystery surrounding the "soviet experiment" fascinated Richard Niebuhr. "The trip to Russia has been one of the events of my life," he wrote back. "I am somewhat dazed by the whole experience."[15] What excited him most was the extent to which this new nation had committed itself to the idea of equality. In Moscow, for example, the unskilled worker paid less rent for a comparable dwelling than a professional person. He was also impressed with the massive construction projects being carried out in the old Russian capital. Here and elsewhere, Niebuhr observed people, as much as the government, displaying a strong will to achieve. The Orthodox church, moreover, only seemed to make the antireligious propaganda of the Communists all the more credible. Although its elaborate rituals and symbols gave refuge to many weary and heavy-laden souls, Niebuhr was convinced that for the most part it remained a grim reminder of the ignorance and superstition of a czarist past.[16]

For the next half decade certain aspects of Marxism continued to attract Niebuhr. He saw a unique kinship between Christianity and the Marxist view of history in particular. Unlike the modern versions of liberalism, both recognized that there were forces in history beyond human control. Both trusted those forces rather than human efforts at social engineering. Both took a hopeful view of the future and believed that out of the misery and discontent of the present order a new world would emerge. In his next major work, *The Kingdom of God in America,* Niebuhr scarcely concealed these feelings. At one point he even argued that the millennialism that flowed from the Great Awakening of the eighteenth century bore a distinct resemblance to the Marxist view. To him, Christians at that time had refrained from confusing the kingdom of God with immediate gratifications and preferred to anticipate its coming more as an "end" that was hastening toward them than as a "goal" they must strive to reach.[17]

---

[14]HRN, "Reformation: Continuing Imperative," *Christian Century* 77 (2 March 1960): 248-51.

[15]HRN to J. H. Horstmann, 5 September 1930, HRN Papers, Eden Theological Seminary Archives.

[16]HRN, "Some Observations on Russia," *Evangelical Herald* 29 (2 October 1930): 795-96; ibid. (9 October 1930): 815-16.

[17]HRN, *The Kingdom of God in America* (New York, 1937) 137.

Such a strategy, he seemed to suggest, commended itself to contemporary Christians concerned about the issues of bread and peace.

Immediately following the sabbatical in Europe, Niebuhr was confronted with perhaps the most important decision in his professional life. With the publication of *Social Sources,* Yale University had recognized him as a scholar of special merit by awarding him a Sterling Fellowship. Then in 1931 he received an appointment to the prestigious faculty of its divinity school. Since his roots were deep in the Evangelical Synod, Niebuhr found it difficult to leave his position at Eden Seminary. At Yale, however, he knew he would find an atmosphere more conducive to broadening his perspective on the Christian church and its mission to the world. The Yale situation was challenging, he wrote shortly after resigning from Eden, because it gave him an "opportunity to deal more directly with the forces that are operating in American theological thought." It also provided a chance to move into the stimulating cultural environment of a great university and to work with graduate students, who in his estimation promised to be more flexible than seminary students in their approach to theology.[18]

At Yale the level of academic expectation was much higher than it was for a professor at Eden. Soon after assuming the new post, Niebuhr began to immerse himself in the writings of such Christian thinkers as Jonathan Edwards, Søren Kierkegaard, and Feodor Dostoyevsky. In his first five years on the faculty he reviewed more than a hundred new books, published several important articles in scholarly journals, and conducted seminars that prepared the ground for his *Kingdom of God in America.* This appetite for achievement was encouraged by a competitive but cordial working relationship with such colleagues as Roland Bainton and Robert L. Calhoun, scholars who were thoroughly versed in the history of Christian thought. Niebuhr seems to have benefited particularly from interchanges with the erudite (but cautious) Calhoun. For nearly three decades these three formed an intellectual triumvirate that gave Yale Divinity School much of its stature.

At the same time, the Yale professorship led to greater opportunities for Niebuhr to interact with theologians and church leaders in the wider Christian community. During the early 1930s he joined Henry P. Van Dusen's "Theological Discussion Group," a gathering of Protestant leaders that met twice a year at Princeton University and the Washington Cathedral's College of Preachers to debate issues in contemporary religious thinking. This group of twenty-five included, besides Bainton and Calhoun, such scholars as Reinhold Niebuhr, Paul Tillich, Walter M. Horton, John C. Bennett, and G. Ernest

---

[18]HRN to T. Lehmann, president of Elmhurst College, 28 January 1931, HRN Papers, Elmhurst College Archives, Elmhurst, Illinois.

Wright. Each two-day meeting was conducted as a seminar. Papers were completed in advance, circulated for study by all participants, and then discussed during the sessions with the aid of a previously appointed critic.

The group also brought Richard Niebuhr into the orbit of "neoorthodoxy." At its meetings various points of view were expressed, but most of the discussions tended to focus on at least one of the five major themes associated with this theological movement: the reaction against modern liberal assumptions about human nature and society, the meaning of a more "realistic" theological outlook, the place of a special revelation in religious knowledge, rethinking the social gospel, and the church as the model of the great community of Christ. Niebuhr's *Church Against the World* grew directly out of his participation in these meetings. Coauthors Pauck, who had quickly established himself as a respected theologian and teacher at the University of Chicago after emigrating from Germany in 1925, and Miller, a Presbyterian layman from Virginia's Shenandoah Valley, were members of the group as well. *The Church Against the World* was just one among the many books that emerged as a result of the meetings of these "younger theologians," as they were called.[19]

Richard Niebuhr's participation in this neoorthodox circle prompts a number of questions. Was he, like so many others associated with neoorthodoxy, a liberal chastened by the disillusionment that became more prominent among American intellectuals with the onset of the Great Depression? To what extent did he call for a return to an older set of Christian beliefs? Did he take the point of view Karl Barth had first begun to articulate in Europe following World War I? In rendering its judgment, the popular mind in America has tended to part the great host of Protestant Christians to the more liberal "left" and the more conservative "right." The dichotomy is one that minorities at both ends of the spectrum have long had a stake in perpetuating. Niebuhr, however, does not really fit at either pole. To see this, one has only to examine the course of his theological development prior to 1931.

2

In working for the Americanization of his Evangelical Synod, Niebuhr shared the conviction of "liberal" Protestants that the wisdom of the Bible had to be adapted to modern thought and culture. This was the approach he first learned from his father. The application of historical criticism to the Bible, Gustav Niebuhr had held, "may have done some good" in forcing Christians to take a "more comprehensive view." In any event, it had "forced the development of Christian thought which otherwise might have remained inert and

---

[19]See Samuel McCrea Cavert, "The Younger Theologians," *Religion in Life* 5 (Fall 1936): 520-31.

stagnant," with the result that "no wide-awake pastor and winner of souls for Christ" could ever consider using the "same methods and measures that had been found useful and adequate sixty years ago."[20] At Union Seminary in New York, Richard Niebuhr's course of study had also pointed him in this direction. Then at Yale he had come under the influence of Frank C. Porter, a professor of biblical theology whose lectures were steeped in the type of liberal scholarship that Albrecht Ritschl and Adolf von Harnack had been setting forth in Europe prior to World War I.[21]

The position was one Niebuhr also took as president of Elmhurst College. "Christian education," he wrote, meant "a thorough acquaintance with contemporary culture, a love of truth, an ability to deal independently with the problems of individual and social life in the light of thorough knowledge, and all shot through with the ideal of Jesus."[22] Elmhurst students, said Niebuhr, should not be protected from the results of historical criticism or the scientific approach to reality. "The interests of scientific education and religious education," Niebuhr told his board of trustees, were not in conflict. It was entirely possible for the school to introduce its students to the world of modern ideas so that they might think as their contemporaries did, make use of the accepted results of scientific research and insight, and yet adhere to the faith and ethics of the gospel. To do otherwise, he continued, would teach students to "evade the problems which Christianity and the Christian face today" and give them "little help if any toward the preservation of [their] own best faith and highest ideals." The best vehicles for religious instruction were courses designed for the promotion of a "Christian attitude toward life" in dealing with social as well as individual problems, he emphasized, not those designed for the "inculcation

---

[20]Gustav Niebuhr, "Modern Methods and Their Application to the Old Gospel Truth," *Messenger of Peace* 12 (15 January 1913): 1.

[21]Liberalism was a major current in American Protestantism for the first three decades of the twentieth century. Its exponents were often heavily influenced by the thinking of such great German scholars as Ritschl and Harnack. Their theological systems were various. Yet it is possible to identify several broad themes articulated by liberals, such as a high estimate of human nature, belief in progress toward a kingdom of God on earth based on an evolutionary view of nature and history, an emphasis on the humanity of Jesus and the immanence of God in humankind and culture, and a stress on ethics. The twin concepts of the fatherhood of God and the brotherhood of man frequently appeared in liberal rhetoric. See William R. Hutchison, ed., *American Protestant Thought: The Liberal Era* (New York, 1968) 1-2; Kenneth Cauthen, *The Impact of American Religious Liberalism* (New York, 1962) 6; William R. Hutchison, *The Modernist Impulse in American Protestantism* (Cambridge MA, 1976) 1-11.

[22]HRN, "The Future of Elmhurst College," in *The Elms* (n.p., 1929) 16.

of doctrines."[23] In seeking to apply these precepts, Niebuhr himself assumed responsibility for new courses that attempted to acquaint the student body with modern philosophical, psychological, and ethical approaches to religion.

In his own teaching and writing Niebuhr interpreted religion in historical terms. Contemporary Christians might read the same words of the New Testament to which the early Christians had harkened, he wrote in 1928, yet they saw no "photographic copy," but at best an "impressionistic attempt at reproduction" of the kingdom Jesus had come to announce. By "making a judicious selection from their heritage," they were in fact as much creators of their own past as people in every age. Their choice, for example, might be the Gospels rather than the letters of Paul favored by the Reformers of the sixteenth century. Also involved, however, were the memories and social connotations of the interpreters themselves. So there were bound to be differences even when it came to interpretations of the same text. According to Niebuhr, the voice of Jesus that spoke to Christians as they turned to Matthew, Luke, and Mark received "more than approval." It gave expression to their own "vague desires, hopes and purposes." Such relativistic features of the gospel, he argued, did not diminish its power. On the contrary, they magnified the extent to which Jesus could be all things to all persons and provide a word of grace sufficient for each person's need.[24]

Having identified himself, at least to this extent, with the liberal movement in American Protestantism, Niebuhr was soon confronting challenges from the more conservative-minded elements in his denomination. One came in 1927 at a conference of Evangelical clergy in Chicago. There Niebuhr in his address tried to update the Christian definition of evil. "While we may not believe in a personal devil, we must certainly agree with the Apostle Paul when he said we reasoned, not with flesh and blood but with powers and principalities." During the open forum that followed, Carl Schaeffer, a theologically conservative pastor, angrily denounced Niebuhr for his "liberal" understanding of the devil and insinuated that the synod was being remiss in allowing someone with such convictions to teach in its schools. Niebuhr was deeply hurt by the remarks, but responded gracefully both to his accuser and to those who rushed to his defense. Evil, he declared, did exist, and God's judgment on evildoers was real; but he rejected the biblical literalism that affirmed the existence of a "personal devil." He had always assumed that toleration of divergent viewpoints was a hallmark of the synod. He disliked having to justify his own in-

[23]HRN, "Report to the Board of Trustees of Elmhurst College," 25 January 1926, p. 4; "Report to the Board of Trustees of Elmhurst College," 31 January 1927, p. 9, HRN Papers, Elmhurst College Archives, Elmhurst, Illinois.

[24]HRN, "The Relativities of Religion," *Christian Century* 45 (18 November 1928): 1456-58.

tegrity. Niebuhr also deplored soft-peddling a position on one issue because it seemed to imply that he denied other classical Christian teachings. And he was deeply concerned with the disruptive effect that a fundamentalist controversy might have on religious education in the synod. "I am very much interested," he said in one of his letters, "in seeing that our educational institutions remain unhampered by the efforts to introduce new standards of orthodoxy, or by the appointment of investigating commissions."[25]

A similar but unrelated controversy occurred in 1929, when Manfred Manrodt, a professor of biblical studies at Eden Seminary, asserted that he had been discharged from his position because his conservative understanding of biblical teachings conflicted with the "modernist" position taken by Dean Niebuhr. Niebuhr, he charged, believed the Bible "contains," instead of "is," the word of God. Not only was Niebuhr teaching the false idea that "salvation" included reform of the social order, but he was seeking to remove faculty members who for this reason were opposed to the union of the synod with the Reformed church. Werner Petersmann, another Eden professor whose teachings were attuned to the renaissance of Luther studies in Germany that followed World War I and to the newer "crisis" theology of Karl Barth, sided with Manrodt. In the heat of the controversy, Reinhold Niebuhr urged his brother to take the offensive and to make the seminary choose the banner under which it wanted to march. Unfortunately, the letter containing this advice from Reinhold was placed by mistake in Manrodt's mailbox, and the disgruntled Eden professor seized the opportunity to reveal its contents to the Saint Louis newspapers.[26]

Once again, Richard Niebuhr found himself on the defensive. In his letter to the seminary's board of directors, he refuted Manrodt's charge of intolerance. "I am too much interested in my own right to freedom in teaching," he wrote, "to wish to deny the same freedom to another." That students might profit more by reading the entire Old Testament in English rather than spending long hours learning Hebrew grammar, he continued, was his only real disagreement with Manrodt. As for Reinhold's part in the controversy, he added, the letter was his brother's way of suggesting that he consider leaving the seminary in order to preserve harmony among faculty members. Richard Niebuhr then offered to submit his resignation. The Eden board was able to blunt the charges against him by maintaining that the elimination of a separate "English

---

[25]HRN to Schaeffer, 10 May 1927; HRN to Rev. Alfred Meyer, 29 April 1927; HRN to H. P. Bloesch, 30 April 1927; HRN to Schaeffer, 29 April 1927, HRN Papers, Eden Theological Seminary Archives. Carl Schneider (interview with author, Webster Groves MO, 1 March 1972) recalls how Niebuhr "broke down" when he was attacked at the Chicago conference for his "liberal" view.

[26]Manrodt Case, Eden Theological Seminary Archives.

Department" from the seminary had necessitated Manrodt's release. It had been purely an administrative decision, the board asserted, to which Niebuhr had not been a party.[27]

Despite his occasional identification with liberal Christianity, Niebuhr held strong reservations about the movement. He never accepted its heady optimism and its unqualified faith in humankind. As a merciless self-critic, early instilled with the classical Christian notions about human sinfulness and its consequences, he conveyed to his colleagues in the synod the impression of a devout Christian who constantly lived in the "passion season" and who was drawn particularly to the meaning of the cross of Christ. Evidence of inexplicable evil and the suffering of the innocent posed questions that he could not dismiss from his thinking. One experience in particular seems to have shaped Richard Niebuhr's outlook. While he was serving as a parish minister in Saint Louis in 1918, a winter outing of Walnut Park's boy scout troop became a disaster. A fish splashing in a small opening on the frozen surface of Creve Coeur Lake attracted the attention of three youths in Niebuhr's company. Unable to contain their curiosity, they ventured out onto the thin ice. But when they reached the hole, the ice gave way, and all three plunged to their deaths. Niebuhr made a frantic effort to save the victims. Chopping wildly at the frigid layers, he severely injured his own hands and arms. Members of Walnut Park Church never forgot the day Pastor Niebuhr conducted the funeral for the three who had drowned. They knew he felt terribly responsible, and they would note that the memory of the experience seemed to diminish his spirit.[28]

Niebuhr also believed that the modernist forms of liberal Christianity lost sight of the objective foundation of faith. This tendency, as he viewed it, became most apparent whenever modernists attempted to wed theology and psychology. At best, the union of the two disciplines promised to demonstrate empirically that human beings were innately religious. More often, theology was subordinated to psychology, and the uniquely spiritual and ethical elements were treated as rationalizations rather than realities. Communion with God in prayer became autosuggestion, revelation a type of religious experience, and God a form of group consciousness or wish fulfillment rather than

---

[27]HRN to the board of directors, Eden Theological Seminary, 3 July 1929; HRN to Rev. John Baltzer, president of the Evangelical Synod of North America, 17 July 1929, HRN Papers, Eden Theological Seminary Archives.

[28]Albert Hoetker, Lillian Schaefer, and Henrietta Swanson, interview with author, St. Louis MO, 1 March 1972. The fact that this memory lingered in Niebuhr's mind was confirmed in my interviews with Carl E. Schneider and Richard R. Niebuhr (Cambridge MA, 21 June 1972).

the object of worship.[29] For this reason, Niebuhr welcomed all signs of a shift toward belief in God as a transcendent reality. In the scientific and philosophical communities, he found these signs in the rejection of a totally mechanistic view of life and an undiminished concern for spiritual values. "Man is not a measure of all things but must be measured by things greater than himself," he asserted in 1927. "Unless we get out of our planetary provincialism, our narrow selfish way of thinking and looking at things, and cultivate a cosmic faith, we can never understand, much less solve the many problems we are facing, nor realize the brotherhood of man."[30]

In theology, Niebuhr found himself attracted to D. C. Macintosh and Karl Barth. In Macintosh he found an "empiricist" who, in probing the experiences of a religious subject, did not fail to acknowledge the reality of the religious object, namely God. Niebuhr's accord with Barth was less complete. As early as 1929 he was convinced that Barth had gone too far in his *Epistle to the Romans.* His wholly transcendent God was too remote from human experience. Yet Niebuhr welcomed the revolt Barth was helping to lead against the anthropocentrism of nineteenth-century religious thought. It helped confirm in him that "religion means not only seeking after God but his self-revelation also, not only pursuit of values but also obedience to the Divine Will, not only striving but trust and assurance, not only the energizing of the will but also its salvation, not only the kingdom of God in its social aspects but also immortality and redemption."[31]

Niebuhr's trip to Europe seems to have reinforced these earlier objections to the optimistic aspects of liberal theology. His mood after his return to the United States was more sober and his observations extremely pessimistic. Christians, he declared in 1931, had only to go to their newspapers, books, and teachers in other fields to learn that the human species was not the godlike creation in whom liberals had placed their confidence, but a race of animal-like savages. Science, he went on to say, had failed to substantiate the idea of continuous biological improvement. Nor had it succeeded in making life richer or happier. The loss of confidence, as he saw it, was reflected as much in the public's skepticism about modern technological innovations as in its more obvious

---

[29]HRN, "Theology and Psychology: A Sterile Union," *Christian Century* 44 (13 January 1927): 47-48; "Jesus Christ Intercessor," *International Journal of Religious Education* 3 (January 1927): 6-8.

[30]HRN, "Planetary Provincialism and Cosmic Faith," quoted in "The Elmhurst Service Conference," *Evangelical Herald* 26 (28 April 1927): 344-45.

[31]HRN, "From the Religion of Humanity to the Religion of God," *Theological Magazine of the Evangelical Synod of North America* 57 (November 1929): 401-409.

cynicism toward government.[32] Weighed in the balance of America's new economic and social woes, Niebuhr seemed to be saying, faith in progress had come up wanting.

At Yale further exposure to Karl Barth along with his reading of Jonathan Edwards served to intensify the accent Niebuhr placed on God as an objective reality. More so than previously, he now depicted the universe as one great system of being in which God was at the center. When illustrating the dynamics of divine sovereignty, his most frequent reference was to Alfred North Whitehead's stages of religion's evolution from "God the void" through "God the enemy" to "God the companion." This implied that faith was a process of coming to believe that the "void" out of which everything in life seemed to emerge and to which it would return was indeed God; of then discovering that this same God was also the "slayer" of all other gods humanity tried to erect and worship; and of concluding that such actions of God in the world were ultimately redemptive in character.[33]

Significant as well was the relationship Niebuhr developed with Paul Tillich. Soon after meeting Tillich in Europe, he translated and furnished a substantial introduction to Tillich's book of 1926, *The Religious Situation.*[34] When Tillich was forced from his teaching post at Frankfurt in 1933, Niebuhr was among those who helped him resettle in the United States. Tillich, on the other hand, helped Niebuhr distinguish his own view of church and world from that of Karl Barth. To some colleagues, at least, Niebuhr's church-against-the-world rhetoric sounded "Barthian."[35] But for Niebuhr, Barth's stress on God's "otherness" had spawned an outlook that saw only depravity in human efforts to alleviate injustice and restricted "salvation" to an eternal realm. In the church, it clearly undercut the sense of social responsibility the gospel demanded of Christians.[36] Tillich, he felt, had worked to bridge this gulf between the divine and the human by maintaining that the infinite appeared as the self-transcending element in everything finite. To bring a religion like Christianity to bear on any human endeavor, therefore, one had only to analyze that endeavor in terms of the "faith" that motivated it. Like Tillich, Niebuhr tended throughout this period to focus on those objects that performed the role of a "god" in people's lives. Faith, he declared, implied loyalty to someone or something that

---

[32]HRN, "Theology in a Time of Disillusionment," HRN Papers, Harvard Divinity School, Cambridge MA.

[33]Alfred North Whitehead, *Religion in the Making* (New York, 1926).

[34]HRN, "Translator's Preface," in Paul Tillich, *The Religious Situation* (New York, 1932) 9-24.

[35]Cavert, "The Younger Theologians," 523, 529.

[36]See HRN, "Theology in a Time of Disillusionment," 19-20.

made life worth living, a "god" who appeared to bestow meaning on existence. Everyone, in his view, lived by faith because everyone made a "god" out of something, be it family, ideology, nation, value system, or whatever else seemed to serve as the source of worthwhile living.[37]

As a corollary to this analysis, Niebuhr employed the classical Christian doctrine of original sin. Sin, as he interpreted it, grew out of the human tendency to worship something other than God, who was the only reality worthy of complete love and trust. Sin meant rebellion against God because sinners organize their lives around an object that draws them away from the true center. Such misplaced loyalty, Niebuhr thought, was the source of all evil in the world, from the disintegration of social relationships to all forms of human cruelty and exploitation of the earth's environment. It also created a predicament from which no human being could ever extricate himself or herself through their own effort. Only a reconciliation initiated by God could provide a way out.[38]

Clearly, then, Richard Niebuhr is a figure to whom interpreters of neoorthodoxy need to pay special attention. Well before the onset of the Great Depression in America, he perceived the gathering theological crisis with which he would be identified in the 1930s. In 1939 the *Christian Century* first ran a series of articles entitled "How My Mind Has Changed in This Decade." While Niebuhr did not contribute to it, thirty-four other religious leaders did. Many of them recalled how they had been compelled to revise their optimistic faith in progress, to become more theological in their outlook, and to reconsider old Christian concepts such as original sin, the sacrificial death of Jesus, and the sovereignty of God.[39] Always difficult to define, neoorthodoxy has been associated most often with this type of transformation. Unlike other Protestant leaders associated with this movement, however, Niebuhr's theological background was not in Protestantism's liberal movement. More than anything else, it was his Evangelical instincts that led him to express serious reservations about the direction of liberal theology and to welcome the signs in America as well as Europe of a new humility about human nature and a resurgence of faith in God. The theological heritage he embraced as a pastor, educator, and leader of his denomination already contained the older Christian themes that neoorthodoxy attempted to reassert. The social and political upheavals of the 1930s were no less shocking to Niebuhr than to others. But their impact was not so much to throw him in a new direction as to confirm a general shift in orien-

---

[37]See HRN, "What Then Shall We Do?" *Christian Century Pulpit* 5 (July 1934): 145-47.

[38]HRN, "Man the Sinner," *Journal of Religion* 15 (July 1935): 272-80.

[39]See *Christian Century* 56 (18 January 1939 to 27 September 1939).

tation to the world that he had in the 1920s urged his own and other Protestant denominations to pursue.

3

"Humanism" was the term Richard Niebuhr chose during the 1930s for his telling indictment of liberal and modernist attitudes toward culture. This false faith, he declared in *The Church Against the World,* rejected not only the Christian symbols of creation, fall, and salvation, but belief in both human frailty and divine atonement through the suffering of the innocent. Its affirmation of the "sufficiency of man" rendered a "second birth" unnecessary. The technological breakthroughs of the twentieth century, he felt, had only reinforced such thinking. Humanists tended to venerate scientific knowledge to the point that they required no other law within the human soul.[40]

A similar malady, as Niebuhr saw it, was at work in the world of capitalism, which seemed to impel people to live within themselves rather than in reference to the transcendent. Their "faith," he argued, called for quick, pragmatic solutions to all problems. Most often, however, it appeared as a desire to control and to dominate all aspects of life. Niebuhr also stressed that capitalist worship of success and efficiency was not restricted to the marketplace; it permeated the politics, the education, the art forms, even the religion of the bourgeoisie.[41] Was it any wonder that the church had become dependent on the flow of gifts from the privileged classes and prone to thinking that capitalist values were Christian ideals? In some cases, he lamented, church members had even defined the church's mission as a crusade to preserve capitalist civilization.[42] While Niebuhr agreed with President Franklin Delano Roosevelt that "the only thing we have to fear is fear itself," he refused to believe that the antidote for fear was the restoration of confidence in American institutions. To him, Roosevelt's homilies glossed over the false faith Americans placed in human self-sufficiency. The president's actions might succeed in controlling or adjusting the depressed economy, but they offered no permanent solution. In Niebuhr's view, a resurgence of faith in God was America's only real hope. From it alone could come the repentance, the sacrifice, and the renewed confidence required for a "new deal."[43]

No less dangerous in Niebuhr's estimation was the fusion of Christianity with any of the radical political alternatives of the 1930s. He knew that the

---

[40]HRN, "Toward the Independence of the Church," in *The Church Against the World,* ed. HRN, 135-37.

[41]HRN, "Translator's Preface," 9-13.

[42]HRN, "Toward the Independence of the Church," 131-32.

[43]HRN, "What Must We Do?" 145-47.

Depression had produced a bumper crop of self-appointed prophets. Huey Long's lieutenant, Gerald L. K. Smith, and Father Charles Coughlin, the radio priest from the Detroit suburb of Royal Oak, had openly denounced the New Deal and gathered substantial national constituencies by championing a "Share-Our-Wealth Society" and setting forth the sixteen points of a "Union for Social Justice." Others, such as those who made policy for the Federal Council of Churches, had advocated a drastically reformed and controlled economy. Still others, including the cutting edge of Protestant idealists and perhaps as many as one of four ministers in the urban Protestant churches of the North, were leaning toward socialism.[44] Niebuhr himself took the uncharacteristically bold step of running (unsuccessfully) on the Socialist ticket for a school board seat in Hamden, Connecticut. But Niebuhr was convinced that to be a Christian and a socialist in politics, one must be more than merely socialist. Christians, to be sure, might join any dissenting group in revolt against the evils in the prevailing order and in commitment to establishing a more just and peaceful way of life. But to think that any such group could create a new order and supply the disinterested persons to rule it was for him the height of messianic delusion. The result of any alliance between Christianity and socialism, he warned, was more likely to be another captivity of the church to culture, or as in Germany, a strong reactionary movement.[45]

At no point did Richard Niebuhr become a Marxist, despite the appeal of both the Marxist view of history and the practical side of the ideology. He especially admired the way Communists could maintain "cell" groups of their followers. Such groups, as he saw it, were loyal to a cause that transcended national and class differences, and they strengthened members in their commitment to that cause. He urged this same "cell" strategy on the church, to strengthen its efforts to transform the world.[46] Yet Marxism in Niebuhr's estimation was simply too materialistic. It openly denied God, immortality, and other transcendent values to which Christians had pledged their allegiance. While Communists were more honest about this than capitalists, they still lacked the Christian capacity for making a repentant evaluation of self. Hence they absolved the proletariat of all responsibility and shifted the blame for society's problems to the ruling classes. "Post-revolutionary" Communism, as he saw it, was different from that which had prompted the revolution. The new ideologies not only tried to "engineer" social improvements as much as mod-

---

[44]See Robert Moats Miller, *American Protestantism and Social Issues, 1919-1939* (Chapel Hill NC, 1958) 62-112.

[45]HRN, "Toward the Independence of the Church," 139-48.

[46]See, for example, HRN, "The Grace of Doing Nothing," *Christian Century* 49 (23 March 1932): 378-80.

ern democratic and fascist states, but they relied on force to accomplish the change.[47] He perceived this tendency in the Stalinist purges of 1936, and it served to diminish the hope he had held out for the Soviet experiment.

Throughout the 1930s Niebuhr took a similar approach to the politics of America's role in world affairs. The ever-darkening clouds of war on both the Eastern and the Western horizons had prompted lively debate, especially among students and faculty at Yale. Many of them, motivated by feelings of guilt about the church's blindly supportive role during World War I, lent their support to the pacifist position. Yet, with the threat of a fascist Germany and Italy and the emergence of a more militant Japan, pacifism was an increasingly difficult position to maintain. Within peace groups such as the Fellowship of Reconciliation (FOR), it led to schism. In Niebuhr's estimation, pacifism was only an inverted form of nationalism. In refusing to soften their opposition to the arms race, the strict pacifists of the FOR were merely substituting reliance on the power of words for faith in military muscle. Economic sanctions seemed to offer them a nonviolent way out. But to him such measures could be just as brutal as any shooting war. Some people might even prefer to be shot rather than starved. Niebuhr also pointed out the "humanist" principles used by the dissenting minority to vindicate their decision to secede from the FOR in 1934. At least this group was being consistent, he wrote. In fact, it was in the name of humanity's good that it was willing to allow the use of force to stem aggression. In the Christian view, however, such aggressiveness on the part of the righteous was just as displeasing to God as that of the unrighteous. On the other hand, the notion that reconciliation came about through a bloody act of crucifixion of the "innocent" made self-sacrifice a demand from which no pacifist was exempted.[48]

Richard and Reinhold Niebuhr disagreed on this issue. The initial focal point of the disagreement was America's response to the Japanese invasion of Manchuria in 1932. The brothers chose to air their difference publicly in three articles that appeared in the *Christian Century*.[49] It seemed at one level that while Richard chose to side with those urging neutrality, Reinhold favored some form of intervention. Actually the disagreement went far deeper. In his book, *Moral Man and Immoral Society,* Reinhold suggested a dichotomy between in-

---

[47]HRN, "The Irreligion of Communist and Capitalist," *Christian Century* 47 (29 October 1930): 1306-1307; also "Faith, Works, and Social Salvation," *Religion in Life* 1 (Fall 1932): 426-30; and "The Grace of Doing Nothing," 379.

[48]HRN, "The Inconsistency of the Majority," *The World Tomorrow* 17 (18 January 1934): 43-44.

[49]HRN, "The Grace of Doing Nothing," 378-80; Reinhold Niebuhr, "Must We Do Nothing?" *Christian Century* 49 (30 March 1932): 415-17; HRN, "A Communication: The Only Way Into the Kingdom of God," *Christian Century* 49 (6 April 1932): 447.

dividual and social ethics and set forth "justice" rather than "love" as the more realistic principle for evaluating issues like the Manchurian crisis.[50] For Richard, such distinctions smacked of the type of entanglement with the world from which Christianity needed to free itself. To him, the kingdom of God could not be sliced into separate realms. Nor could the ethics associated with it be compromised. In every situation, Richard believed, the church must assert the full implications of the divine threat of judgment and the gospel promise of redemption. If Americans were to plunge into the Manchurian crisis, they were likely to fool themselves into self-righteousness; detachment, on the other hand, might lead them to repent of the imperialistic greed that was still motivating so much of their foreign policy.

On principle, Reinhold found himself in agreement with this facet of Richard's argument. "It is literally true," wrote Reinhold, "that every recalcitrant nation, like every anti-social individual, is created by the society which condemns it." And "redemptive efforts which betray strong ulterior motives are always bound to be less than fully redemptive." Yet he charged his brother with being too naive, too willing to assume that Americans or anyone else could save the world by aspiring to repent of self-interest. Repentance, said Reinhold, might limit the strife between peoples in history, but it would never succeed in abolishing it. If Japan were to be dissuaded from its military adventurism, force might also need to be used.

In reply, Richard emphasized that the Manchurian crisis still posed an "either-or" question. To amend repentance with the self-assertive behavior his brother condoned remained a "hopeless compromise" of Christian ideals. The kingdom of God, he also warned, would never grow in the soil that Reinhold was preparing. His brother's way could produce only a never ending jungle of assertions and counterassertions that would keep the world on the brink of war.

At issue as well for Richard Niebuhr was his brother's utilitarian approach to problem solving. In another article from 1932 Richard argued persuasively that the heretical notion of "salvation by works" was the common denominator of modern fascist, democratic, and socialist societies. All trusted humanity's ability to reason and to master its own fate. All employed social engineering techniques to improve society. Eighteenth- and nineteenth-century versions of liberal democracy, he stressed, had come much closer to the more theologically accurate notion of "salvation by faith." In those societies, people did not try to control nature or to manipulate the future. Nor were they as prone to bondage to capitalist and nationalist ideologies. Instead, they trusted that God was both above and working through history. Although this article did not mention

---

[50]Reinhold Niebuhr, *Moral Man and Immoral Society* (New York, 1932).

Reinhold by name, it clearly refuted his willingness to rely on America's ability to manipulate Japan into withdrawing from Manchuria.[51]

All in all, the debate reveals how deeply both Niebuhrs were involved in the neoorthodox reaction to liberalism's faith in progressive cultural improvement. Richard emphasized this in an apparent attempt to smooth over the rough edges of their disagreement. Privately, he gave Reinhold a younger brother's respect and praised *Moral Man and Immoral Society* as one of the two most significant books published since the end of World War I.[52] Yet of the two, Reinhold appears to have owed more to that against which he rebelled. His celebrated distinction between "justice" and "love" in *Moral Man and Immoral Society* was not so much a deviation from the liberal outlook as an attempt to make that outlook more realistic or practical. Not until such later works as *The Nature and Destiny of Man* did his view of humankind assume a more orthodox mold. In fact, this change of mind was one to which Richard's criticisms had made no small contribution.

4

Despite his persistent indictment of "humanism," Richard Niebuhr remained true to his earlier commitment to social Christianity. At Yale he took the position that the chaos of the Great Depression had mounted a crisis of faith that called for a strategic "withdrawal" rather than a redoubling of previous efforts to invade society. Only in this way, he believed, could the church reassert its loyalty to God and to Jesus Christ. Yet for him, "withdrawal" never implied world-fleeing asceticism. On the contrary, it was only a temporary measure, undertaken for the sake of a new aggression and participation in the world.

In *The Church Against the World* Niebuhr called "withdrawal" the first step in a recurring cycle that organized Christianity had repeated three times in its history: the first withdrawal occurred when the formalized rituals and institutions of the third century replaced the living faith of the apostles; the second, when scholasticism had halted the religious renaissance of the twelfth and thirteenth centuries; the third, at the close of the Reformation, as state churches emerged throughout Europe to defend pure doctrine and conventional morality. The modern church, he was convinced, had come to yet another such point. The easy identification of Christianity with Western culture had led to its captivity to such worldly faiths as capitalism, nationalism, and humanism. The disillusionment with democracy, the loss of confidence in the scientific com-

---

[51]HRN, "Faith, Works, and Social Salvation," 426-30.

[52]HRN to Reinhold Niebuhr, n.d., Reinhold Niebuhr Papers, Library of Congress, Washington DC.

munity, and the state of helplessness into which liberal Protestantism had sunk all pointed to the same truth. The pain and the disruptions of the Depression were regrettable, but they were necessary in order to bring about the redemption of both Christianity and culture.[53]

Niebuhr's real intention becomes even more apparent as one examines the theology undergirding his view of history. As early as 1932 he contrasted the Hebrew and Greek views of time and the world. While the "Jewish gospel" saw God at work in the process of history as a whole and heaven as a new creation for entire nations and peoples, the "Greek gospel" depicted God as an eternal being beyond history and the soul's redemption as deliverance from its material bondage. Both, he declared, perceived life's discontinuities and accented the necessity of a "second birth." Both ran counter to the humanistic thrust of liberal Protestantism. Yet there was an all-important difference in their attitudes toward the world. Christians who took a Hebrew view of things did not deny the "physical" world but only the self-centered perversions and distortions of life in it. For them, the world was neither as transient nor as intrinsically bad as the Greeks held. Rather, it was always subject to divine redemption.[54]

This "Jewish gospel" was the one to which Niebuhr was clearly more attracted: it was not only better attuned to America's philosophical and religious heritage, but it was also more applicable to the problems of his own day. In the debate with his brother, he asserted that the Manchurian crisis was in fact a revelation of divine judgment, the bitter fruit of the seeds of self-interest the Western nations had sown. "Inactivity" on America's part, he argued, did not reflect the moral indignation and frustration of pacifist groups. Rather, it stemmed from the penitent recognition that the outcome of this "judgment of the world" was not affected by human desire for different results. Like the Marxists, Niebuhr believed that redemption required the death of the old way of doing things. Only then was there a chance for a new world order to be born.[55]

The assumptions behind such assertions pose difficult philosophical questions. Is God the only ruler in the universe? Does God cause or permit tragic events? To what extent may divine ideals be applied to human affairs? For Richard Niebuhr some of the most rigorous questioning came from his brother Reinhold in 1932. Reinhold saw no real prospect of squaring the will of God with the immediate realities of conflict in history. "Man's reach is beyond his

---

[53]HRN, "Toward the Independence of the Church," 123-28.

[54]HRN, "Greeks, Jews and Americans in Christ," *Keryx* 23 (March 1932): 3-4, 12.

[55]HRN, "The Grace of Doing Nothing," 378-80. See also HRN, "Christianity and World Problems," *Report of the Fifth National Convention of the Evangelical Women's Union, "Facing World Problems with Christ," Buffalo, New York, June 27-30, 1933*, pp. 85-88.

grasp," he quipped, "or what's a heaven for?" Here on earth, nations such as the United States were better off seeking pragmatic solutions to their problems. He also felt that his brother's understanding of history identified everything that occurred with the "counsels of God" and left the impression that God used actions and forces that humanity could only regard as immoral to establish a more ideal society. As Reinhold saw it, history held out no such promise. All that the world had reason to expect was "perennial tragedy."[56] In response, Richard asserted that his brother was trying to separate God from history. God was "always in history," he contended, as "the structure of things, the source of all meaning, the 'I am that I am,' that which is that it is." God was both enemy and redeemer of the world, heaping judgment on all self-assertive behavior, yet bringing about the good. To the extent that they had brought such evils as economic depression or war upon themselves, fathers could expect God to visit their iniquity upon their children. Such judgment was not simply punitive. God pruned the human tendency to act selfishly in order to revive the possibility of a better world, one more consistent with the divine ideal.[57]

Niebuhr's evaluation of the social gospel followed a similar pattern of development. The movement's chief problem during the 1930s, as he saw it, was not its social concern, but the liberal theology undergirding it. He recognized that liberal Christianity had helped the churches to set forth the Christian hope in ethical terms. But the modernist theology "seemed totally inadequate to account for the toughness, the resistant power, the tremendous inertia of sin in social character." Too often, he believed, its preachers had ensconced themselves in comfortable middle-class pulpits, where their aim was to make Christianity more intellectually palatable rather than to present the Bible's "devastating judgment" on the evils of modern industrialization and warfare. The liberal doctrine of progress failed to sound the note of "imperativeness" Christians found in both the gospel and the actual needs of their society.[58]

Just as inadequate was the Christology of the movement's more recent leaders. In a paper Niebuhr presented in 1933 at a meeting of the American Theological Society, he analyzed the works of Walter Rauschenbusch, Francis Greenwood Peabody, Shailer Matthews, Harry Ward, Kirby Page, Justin Wroe Nixon, and Reinhold Niebuhr, and asserted that liberalism had distorted the New Testament portrait of Jesus. The chief culprit, he declared, was the liberal tendency to make human values determinative for assessing everything, in-

---

[56]Reinhold Niebuhr, "Must We Do Nothing?" 416-17.

[57]HRN, "A Communication: The Only Way into the Kingdom of God," 447.

[58]HRN, "The Social Gospel and Liberal Theology," *Keryx* 22 (May 1931): 12-13, 18.

cluding God. Jesus in fact possessed a God-centered outlook along with the mind of a revolutionary strategist. He was as much a prophet of doom as an ethical teacher. Niebuhr acknowledged that the liberal view of Jesus had accented properly the love of God. But for him it failed to arouse enough of the fear and repentance on which any renewal of the gospel's social power must certainly depend.[59]

Niebuhr maintained that social gospel programs had also failed because they had banked on "indirect" means of achieving their objectives. They had aimed to influence legislatures, to use political parties and schools, to work through the labor movement. But all such efforts, as he saw it, seemed to presuppose that religion had no real bearing on life, that politics and economics provided a more prophetic mode of analysis, that the salvation of society could be achieved by the "works" of its own members. "God in this theory," he explained, "becomes a means to an end; he is there for the sake of achieving a human ideal and he does not do this even directly but only through the inspiration which he offers to those who worship him."[60]

What Niebuhr was moving toward throughout this period was the wedding of the social gospel to a new theology. From the beginning, he ruled out fundamentalism as a prospective partner.[61] In neoorthodoxy he saw more compatibility. Its uncompromising doctrine of original sin could be used to put social injustices into a sharper relief.[62] Furthermore, in its theocentric perspective on the world, salvation was a process requiring human adjustments to the ways of God in history as revealed in the event of Jesus Christ. Its approach to social problems was also "direct" enough to attack the mammonisms and the nationalisms in which society had mistakenly placed its trust.[63]

At one point, Niebuhr even ventured to match up the social gospel with Barthianism. He still recognized the extent of the havoc Barth had created among socially minded Protestants. Barth had clearly portrayed God as issuing an emphatic "no" to all human efforts to construct earthly kingdoms of love and brotherhood. Yet these negations, as Niebuhr saw it, reflected Barth's dialectical method of theologizing. Barth was in fact asserting that God alone

---

[59]HRN, "The Social Gospel and the Mind of Jesus," unpublished essay read before the American Theological Society, New York, 21 April 1933, HRN Papers, Harvard Divinity School; see also "Value Theory and Theology," in *The Nature of Religious Experience,* ed. Julius Seelye Bixler, Robert L. Calhoun, and Helmut Richard Niebuhr (New York, 1937) 93-116.

[60]HRN, "The Attack Upon the Social Gospel," *Religion in Life* 5 (Spring 1936): 176-81.

[61]HRN, "The Social Gospel and Liberal Theology," 13.

[62]Ibid.

[63]HRN, "The Attack Upon the Social Gospel," 180-81.

could establish the kingdom, disclose its purpose through the revelation of Christ, and determine the kind of improvement Christians might strive to make in the world.[64]

It was in the older tradition of American evangelicalism, however, that Niebuhr found the most appealing partner for the social gospel. As early as 1930 he pointed out that the social gospel movement had degenerated into a program of pure activism because it had lost touch with the faith and piety of early leaders like Rauschenbusch and Gladden.[65] Again in 1936 he saw parallels between neoorthodox and evangelical theologies. The former, he wrote, "must not be interpreted as reactions to Evangelical individualism, but as efforts to discover in our own day the social equivalent of the Evangelical strategy."[66] A year later, these observations coalesced into the underlying theme of his book, *The Kingdom of God in America.*

5

Like *Social Sources,* this work of 1937 may be read in several different ways. On the one hand, Niebuhr was offering the world a fresh interpretation of American Christianity. His earlier sociological approach, he explained in the preface to the new book, had left him "dissatisfied" at a number of points. It explained how currents of the American religious "stream" flowed in particular "channels," but did not account for the force of the stream itself. Neither did it attend to those aspects of faith that stood independently of culture and that were aggressive rather than passive, molding culture instead of being molded by it.[67] The time had come, he declared, to look at history from a theological perspective that would account for Christianity's power over the culture.

The new perspective also took issue with the framework such liberal historians as Vernon Parrington had employed to interpret America's past. Niebuhr agreed that the Puritans had seen America as an "experiment in constructive Protestantism," an opportune place, that is, to complete the Reformation that had foundered in Europe.[68] But he insisted that leaders like William Bradford, John Winthrop, and William Penn were neither early proponents of the American dream nor visionaries filled with utopian fantasies

---

[64]HRN, "The Kingdom of God and Eschatology (Social Gospel and Barthianism)," essay presented to the Theological Discussion Group, n.d., HRN Papers, Yale Divinity School, New Haven CT.

[65]HRN, "Can German and American Christians Understand Each Other?" *Christian Century* 47 (23 July 1930): 914.

[66]HRN, "The Attack Upon the Social Gospel," 181.

[67]HRN, *Kingdom of God in America,* ix-x.

[68]Ibid., 17-44.

about establishing the kingdom of God on earth. On the contrary, they were realists, persons who spoke of grim realities, not high-flown plans. While they hoped that their faith would produce a righteous people, they did not base that hope on utopian assumptions about humankind. Instead, the doctrine of original sin shaped their thought, convincing them that since the human mind was darkened, social conflict was inevitable. For them, the kingdom of God implied divine judgment of persons, nature, and history, not an ideal realized through human efforts.[69]

No better example of this revisionist approach might be given than Niebuhr's interpretation of Jonathan Edwards. At the time, social historians had portrayed the work of this eighteenth-century divine as the dead hand of the past holding back an America that was moving into a more liberal future. Niebuhr, on the other hand, took the position that the Great Awakening represented a new emphasis. Its greatest appeal in fact was to those Americans whose developing sense of freedom from intellectual and political constraints was beginning to match the economic independence the New World had bequeathed to them. Edwards's hell-fire sermons, he argued, were anchored in his conviction of the absolute sovereignty of God. "Sinners in the Hands of an Angry God" was far from being a shabby device to frighten or wheedle people into obedience to conventional morality. Rather, it was Edwards's way of summoning them to "press into" the kingdom he believed was near. It reflected his "intense awareness of the precariousness of life's poise, of the utter insecurity of men and of mankind which are at every moment as ready to plunge into the abyss of disintegration, barbarism, crime and the war of all against all, as to advance toward harmony and integration." Balancing this threat was the promise which in Edwards's preaching held out the possibility of a new world, a future that Christ's followers could anticipate and at least partially bring into the present. For Edwards, Niebuhr emphasized, the character of this promise was both social and progressive. It included blessings such as peace, prosperity, health, and long life.[70]

America's religious history was clearly Niebuhr's backdrop for further reflection and clarification of his own thoughts on church and world. In *The Church Against the World,* he had taken issue with Christianity's external critics. Since they were not committed to the church—their criticisms were gauged not by Christian faith in God, but by that of the world—they demanded that it become a "savior" of society rather than "the company of those who have

[69]Ibid., 46-51.

[70]Ibid., 135-45.

found a savior." God could use these critics as instruments of judgment, he conceded, but their intention remained foreign to the real nature of the church.[71]

Similarly, in his introduction to *The Kingdom of God,* Niebuhr insisted that Christianity in America must be interpreted "out of itself." One must discover the pattern within it, and avoid superimposing some other pattern upon it. For him, this pattern necessarily encompassed Christianity's "prophetic strain," its summons to rebirth, its announcements of divine judgment, and its anticipations of God's salvation. To discern the pattern, he contended, one must view Christianity as a dynamic movement, stand "within it," and adopt, at least provisionally, the presuppositions, the fundamental faith on which it rested.[72] In the chapters that followed, he described this movement as a progressive unfolding of God's sovereign love and will to establish a coming kingdom.

The Kingdom of God featured those Christians from America's past who had restored the church to integrity by "withdrawal" from the world. Niebuhr compared the Puritans and the evangelicals to the mendicant orders of the high Middle Ages. For John Cotton and Roger Williams, he stressed, the church was the "ecclesia," an assembly or movement of people called out of the "pluralism" and the "temporalism" of the world to loyalty to God as the supreme reality and only good. He thought Williams was the "most otherworldly man of all the New Englanders, a Protestant monk" who wrestled with the great question of how any human organization might serve as a pure expression of the divinely established church. Cotton Mather, on the other hand, seemed to him to have succumbed to the old temptation to confuse the established order with the kingdom of God. Mather reduced the dynamic message of the gospel to a set of moral laws to be studied in a state of "hypochondriac introspection."[73] Jonathan Edwards and the other revivalists of the eighteenth century, as Niebuhr saw them, broke the fetters of this "petrified Puritanism," revived faith in a sovereign God, and, like the Franciscans of the Middle Ages, formed a series of religious orders that insured the victory of the newly converted church over the worldliness of its society.[74]

Niebuhr also continued his critique of humanism in *The Kingdom of God.* When he analyzed the Great Awakening, for instance, he claimed that this false faith or any other altruistic form of love of neighbor was not the essence of its new religion of the heart. The revivalists, he asserted, clearly recognized the unreliability of idealism that remained bound to self-interest and the futility of

---

[71]HRN, "The Question of the Church," 3-4.

[72]HRN, *Kingdom of God in America,* 9-15.

[73]Ibid., 67-69, 170-72.

[74]Ibid., 110-12, 119-20, 172.

depending on the power of one's own will to generate change. For Jonathan Edwards, "true virtue" required that God redirect the human will. He and his colaborers defined love of neighbor in terms of love of God; apart from that, all was sentimentality—only an extension of self-love. The colonial revivalists exhorted their audiences to love other persons, not because of the intrinsic worth of their personalities, but because they were creatures of God and sacred by virtue of their relationship to the God whom Jesus Christ had shown to be seeking their redemption. Likewise, the evangelical leaders of the Second Great Awakening, in calling for temperance, peace, prison reform, and the alleviation of poverty, had not based their humanitarian enterprises on the principle of human goodness as their contemporaries, the "humanist democrats," did. Instead, they had rallied around the ideal of the kingdom of Christ, and proclaimed a God-given "second birth" that liberated persons and enabled them to follow a revolutionary way of life, through Christ. As Niebuhr himself put it, "For America it was a new beginning; it was our national conversion."[75]

At the same time Niebuhr emphasized the strong sense of social responsibility that the evangelical revivalists had helped to create. In their minds, he argued, the effects of the coming kingdom of God were as much social as personal. Charles G. Finney, to be sure, had insisted that hastening the final consummation of the kingdom of God involved personal conversions to Christ rather than reform measures. Yet he had maintained that persons converted and reconciled to God must bring forth fruits of righteousness in actual social life.[76] In Niebuhr's estimation, social gospel patriarchs like Samuel Harris, Washington Gladden, and Walter Rauschenbusch had employed this same strategy. For them, the social gospel clearly implied neither a rationalism that looked upon the cross and resurrection as ancient superstitions nor a liberalism that denied the sovereignty of God, but a faith that was never ashamed of the gospel of Christ.[77]

As in Niebuhr's other writings from the 1930s, the real object of his criticisms in *The Kingdom of God* was not the social gospel, but the liberal theology that had supplanted its evangelical rationale. The indictment for which the book is perhaps best remembered is often quoted out of context. The statement, "A God without wrath brought men without sin into a kingdom without judgment through the ministrations of a Christ without a cross," in its proper context actually condemned the fatal transformation Niebuhr ascribed to the evangelical side of American Protestantism. In the middle of the nineteenth century,

---

[75]Ibid., 99-116.

[76]Ibid., 155-56.

[77]Ibid., 160-63.

he conceded, protoliberal leaders such as William Ellery Channing, Ralph Waldo Emerson, and Horace Bushnell had remained akin to the evangelicals in their thinking. They had continued to look for the regeneration of the whole person rather than certain aspects of one's moral behavior and to ground any belief in "progress" in a Hebrew-Christian reading of history. Yet change had occurred when their successors lost sight of the discontinuities between God and humanity, confused the church with the world, and narrowed the focus of the coming of Christ's kingdom from a radical revolution to those religious capacities of humankind that Jesus the teacher might further develop.[78]

Like other members of the neoorthodox movement in America, then, Richard Niebuhr was repulsed by the "world" in the church of the 1930s. He was clearly determined to emphasize the prophetic element in Christianity, to repudiate its identification with all cultural ideologies, and to reassert the meaning of faith in God. Nevertheless, he continued to focus on the responsibilities of Christians to the world and to feature the "this-worldly" hopes and concerns of evangelical Protestants that had given rise to the social gospel. Both of these themes not only reflect positions he had taken during his early years in the Evangelical Synod, but were set forth in the *The Kingdom of God* as recurrent features of America's religious history. The World War that followed on the heels of the Great Depression only exacerbated Niebuhr's struggle to incorporate his church-world accents on "identification" and "withdrawal" into a single strategy.

---

[78]Ibid., 184-93.

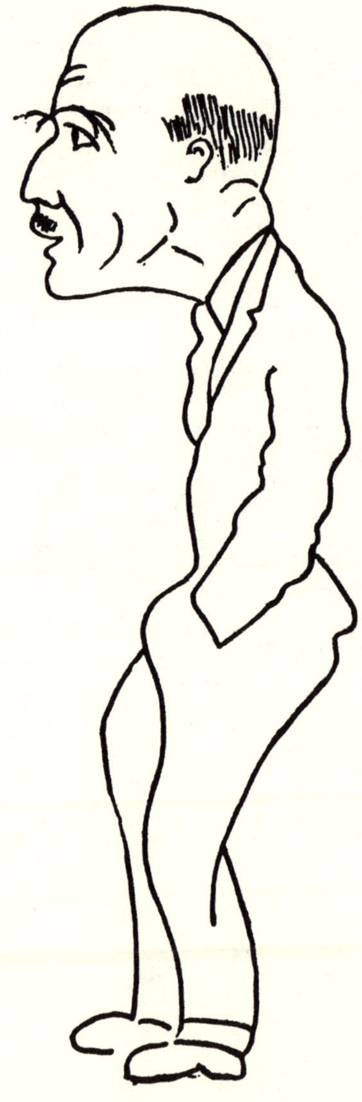

Cartoon by Roland Bainton
(Courtesy Roland Bainton)

CHAPTER III

World War and Democracy

"It is the church's duty to point out the real, not the superficial issues, and to lead men and nations to the ultimate decision, which is not the decision of war or peace but of American peace or peace of God, American war or acceptance of the judgment of God."

H. Richard Niebuhr
"The Christian Church and the World's Crisis," 17

World War II was a difficult period in the life of Richard Niebuhr. As early as 1939 he identified the contemporary church with Jesus' followers in the Garden of Gethsemane. Like them, he declared, Christians might be tempted to grow weary and allow the "agony of China" or the "crucifixion of the Jews" in Europe to dull them into fatalistic resignation. As at other times, therefore, Christians needed to recall the prayer of Jesus and learn that the cure for such "sleep" lay in "wrestling with God" and in waiting to see at least a fragment of the divine plan for the world.[1] "I am convinced," Niebuhr wrote in 1941, "that our whole social world needs to undergo a transformation of the profoundest sort before it can participate in the fully realized plan of God for the world of men." Christians in particular, he thought, had lost sight of the coming of the kingdom of God as an event involving as much judgment as glory, both crucifixion and resurrection, a pilgrimage through the "valley of the shadow" as well as an entrance into the "house of the Lord." In times past, moments of goodness and wisdom were frequent enough to make one want to believe in God's rule over all things. But in "these moments of the world's tragedy," he confessed, only God could wring such faith from people, including himself.[2]

[1]H. Richard Niebuhr (hereafter cited as HRN), "Two Lenten Meditations: 'Tired Christians' and 'Preparation for Maladjustment,' " *Yale Divinity News* 25 (March 1939): 3-4

[2]HRN, "I Believe in the Kingdom of God," *Youth* 4 (12 January 1941): 3-4.

Pearl Harbor and America's entry into the war became a further source of deep anguish for Niebuhr. As disturbing to him as Hitler's holocaust were such Allied policies as "strategic bombing" and "unconditional surrender." For his sermon texts, therefore, he frequently drew on the Old Testament story of Job, such apocalyptic portions of the New Testament as Mark 13, and the Book of Revelation. He struggled time and again to reconcile his faith in the sovereignty of God with the evils of modern warfare and the slaughter of its innocent victims.[3]

Several personal crises only compounded this load. Particularly painful for Niebuhr was the unhappy marriage and divorce of his daughter Cynthia. Fathers in every age have weathered such storms. But for a person of Niebuhr's sensitivity and position, this one came as the severest of blows.[4] In 1944 Niebuhr also turned fifty years of age and thus came face to face with the anniversary of his own father's death. The fact that Gustav Niebuhr's life had come to an end at this same early age became a preoccupation that aroused feelings of unworthiness and guilt. As James Fowler has pointed out, Richard Niebuhr's agonizing over this and other matters helped drive him into a "virtually paralyzing depression" that necessitated a period of hospitalization.[5]

Yet ultimately the entire ordeal seems to have galvanized Niebuhr's reflections on church and world. His views of World War II and the ensuing Cold War years reveal how the nationalist aspects of America's involvement in those events drove him to take issue with all who sought to identify democratic institutions with Christianity. Niebuhr felt that the church must help America see the redemptive hand of God in war as well as peace, but at the same time it must assert that its faith transcended the nation's self-interest. Niebuhr's efforts to develop this position yielded an important set of fresh insights into the relationship between America's religious and democratic traditions.

1

First signs of Niebuhr's concern surfaced during the stormy isolationist-interventionist debates that erupted following the outbreak of war in Europe in 1939. Along with most Americans, church leaders like him tended to iden-

---

[3]See HRN, "The Shape of Things to Come," a baccalaureate sermon, Connecticut College, 5 June 1943; three chapel addresses on "Christ's Vision of Evil," n.d. (but obviously from this period); a sermon on Job 40: 1-9 and 42: 1-6 (one in which he made "unconditional surrender" the focus of his concern); two chapel addresses given on 3 July and 5 July 1945, HRN Papers, Harvard Divinity School, Cambridge MA.

[4]Professor Waldo Beach, interview with author, Durham NC, 15 June 1982.

[5]James W. Fowler, *To See the Kingdom: The Theological Vision of H. Richard Niebuhr* (Nashville, 1974) 5.

tify with the cause of the Allies against Nazi Germany. But they registered sharp differences of opinion over the specific course of action that the government should take. Consistent advocates of pacifism such as A. J. Muste, for instance, rejected any form of intervention, called for unilateral disarmament, and hoped for the creation of an effective world government. Others, particularly those who sided with Charles Clayton Morrison of the *Christian Century,* tended to favor a negotiated peace, bitterly attacked President Roosevelt's more sweeping efforts to make America into an "arsenal of democracy," and appeared to take the side of isolationists like Charles Lindbergh. For these "noninterventionists," as Donald Meyer has described them, what had made America a "chosen nation," more righteous and moral than others, could be preserved only through detachment from European affairs.[6] Still others, including Reinhold Niebuhr and those who joined him in establishing a new periodical, *Christianity and Crisis,* became convinced that world peace and order required that totalitarian aggression be halted. Like the "internationalists" in Congress, they endorsed a policy of all-out aid to the Allies.

Richard Niebuhr found fault with both the isolationist and the interventionist positions. In seeking to defend America, both groups were making "democracy" an object of religious devotion. He voiced this concern most forcefully in a lecture at Berkeley Divinity School in 1940, asserting that insofar as Christianity meant faith in the God whom Jesus Christ had revealed to humanity, it was indifferent to all forms of government. God still ruled and summoned Christ's followers to obey God's will as much within monarchies and oligarchies as democracies. Such obedience, to be sure, always implied opposition to human absolutism; in a democracy, this meant resistance to any attempt to make the popular will the final authority in society. Christian faith in God also encouraged participation in the political process as a means of expressing concern for the welfare of others. It pressed the state to treat all persons as equals and demanded that it protect the liberties of even those who disagreed with its aims. Such political actions, however, did not prove that Christianity was a democratic religion. According to Niebuhr, they manifested only the Christian pursuit of the will of God in a democratic context.[7]

Did foreign policy decisions call for a Christian prescription of the specific policy America was to follow? In Niebuhr's estimation, the church's role was to bring its theological perspective to bear on the policy-making process itself and thus help the nation to become morally fit for any decision it might be

---

[6]Donald B. Meyer, *The Protestant Search for Political Realism, 1919-1941* (Berkeley, 1961) 375-85.

[7]HRN, "The Relation of Christianity and Democracy," Earl Lecture, Berkeley Divinity School, October 1940, HRN Papers, Harvard Divinity School.

required to make. Prior to Pearl Harbor, his most explicit statement of this position came in an address to the Fellowship of Socialist Christians, a group that was deeply divided by the isolationist-interventionist debate. The real issue, he told them, was not the question of staying at peace or going to war, but the motive behind the decision: whether to protect America's own prosperity, righteousness, and independence, or to guard the liberties of small nations and to accept full responsibility for maintaining order in the world. To see the issue this way, one had only to identify the "context" in which both sides couched their rhetoric. Here they would discover that the real clash was between "universal" and "nationalist" religious faiths, that the real choices were "American peace" or "peace of God" and "American war" or "acceptance of the judgment of God."[8]

As part of this same struggle, Niebuhr was clearly groping for a more satisfactory approach to church-state issues. *Social Sources of Denominationalism* contained his earliest assessments of how the religious freedom guaranteed by the First Amendment to the Constitution had affected the churches. Niebuhr found that it had forced "church" type immigrant groups to adopt the sectarian principle of voluntary church membership, to employ evangelistic techniques stressing personal appropriation of religious faith, to make representative forms of self-government the model for their polity. Stripped from all such groups in the New World were the trappings that had linked them with monarchs and princes and allowed them to interfere with the legislative functions of the state. "Sect" type groups, on the other hand, had learned to become more supportive of the state and its causes, especially in time of war.[9] In America, Niebuhr subsequently explained, sectarian groups had not isolated themselves but had formed close relationships with Jeffersonian and Jacksonian democrats. In fact, the evangelical revivals had taken hold where democratic fervor was the strongest; they also helped nurture the social reforms of the national period.[10] More often, however, democracy had tended to bolster repeated victories of the world over the church. By keeping church and state separate, it had made all denominations intensely competitive. Under the influence of the Tractarian movement, for example, the Episcopal church had reversed its long-standing ecumenical approach to other denominations. Here, as elsewhere, the democratic "right" to disagree with competitors produced an essentially worldly corruption of a major Christian impulse.[11]

---

[8]H. Richard Niebuhr, "The Christian Church in the World's Crisis," *Christianity and Society* 6 (Summer 1941): 11-17.

[9]HRN, *The Social Sources of Denominationalism* (New York, 1929) 205-11.

[10]*Encyclopedia of the Social Sciences* (New York, 1931) s.v. "sects."

[11]HRN, *Social Sources of Denominationalism*, 217-34.

In 1937 Niebuhr singled out several areas in which the Protestant accent on the sovereignty of God had helped make Americans more democratic. His strongest argument in *The Kingdom of God in America* concerned the power of governments. As he saw it, the passionate loyalty colonial Christians gave to God sharpened their determination to restrain any human abuse of power. Suspicious of the power of all governments, they had become inclined toward a system in which the power to rule was dispersed and subjected to checks and balances. Subsequently, America's founders made this principle of the limitation of power the cornerstone of the republic. Niebuhr stated that Lord Bryce was "probably right" in suggesting that the Constitution was the work of persons who believed in the idea of original sin. They understood that a government given the power to do wrong would exercise that power. Even in a democracy, they believed, the rights of minorities had to be protected from the potential tyranny that the majority might choose to exercise.[12]

For Niebuhr, then, the idea of a wall of separation between church and every affair of state represented faulty thinking. It reflected Thomas Jefferson's deistic views that each person was a sovereign being, that religious dogmatism was a form of tyranny, and that religious liberty was an effective means of nullifying the power of the church. But it was not the line of reasoning James Madison had employed in advocating the First Amendment to the Constitution. His was the Calvinist belief that since absolute power belonged to God, the power of any human being or institution within the created order of the universe must be limited. According to Niebuhr, Madison's view of religious liberty placed a definite "check" on the power of government. It served to remind all Americans that duties owed to God were always prior to their obligations as citizens of the state.[13]

For the church, as Niebuhr now saw it, "withdrawal" was no longer plausible as a strategy. Christianity, he asserted in 1939, was not a set of "supercultural" truths radically opposed to culture. Nor did it call for "anticultural asceticism." Its chief purpose was to expose the finite, the perverse, the idolatrous features of life in the world. Even in doing this, he conceded, the church could only employ the prevailing cultural philosophy as its vehicle of proclamation.[14]

At the same time Niebuhr was reexploring "The Reformers' Ideal of the Church in the World." Luther and Calvin, he argued, could not foresee the cultural churches into which modern Christendom would become divided.

---

[12]HRN, *The Kingdom of God in America* (New York, 1937) 75-80.

[13]HRN, "The Limitation of Power and Religious Liberty," address to the Institute of Human Relations at Williamstown MA, 27 August 1939, HRN Papers, Harvard Divinity School.

[14]HRN, "The Christian Evangel and Social Culture," *Religion in Life* 8 (Fall 1939): 44-48.

Nevertheless, they had decisively resisted the temptation of the church to become "of the world." In Niebuhr's terms, neither Reformer dreamed of an eternal Wittenberg or Geneva. Rather, both viewed the sad mortality of all utopias as a testimony to the sole sufficiency of faith in God. On the other hand, both had parted company with the medieval mystics and monks because they were "realists," individuals, that is, who knew that they together with the rest of humankind were sinners. Both Reformers refused to place themselves above the law of God or to use that law to judge others because, as Niebuhr explained it, they recognized that the church was as subject to corruption and idolatry as the world. For both, God's reign encompassed the secular as well as the sacred areas of life; as part of the church, they were convinced of their God-given duty to help restrain evil in the world and to root out wickedness in places of high as well as low degree. With such concepts as the "priesthood of all believers" and "vocation," they returned the church to the world, where they reforged its ideals under the hammer of God's word.[15]

2

The "world" of the early 1940s, however, was at war. In fact, Niebuhr found that the events of this entire period posed a much stiffer test for his view of God's role in world history than anything his brother Reinhold had offered during their debate over the Manchurian crisis. His struggle with this issue is prominent in three important theological essays he published in the *Christian Century*.[16] In the first of these, entitled "War as the Judgment of God," Niebuhr set forth his contention that the war's allies and enemies alike stood convicted of the sin of self-centeredness. In America's case, it took the form of a "profound preoccupation with its own prosperity, safety and righteousness." Rather than assume responsibility for its neighbors in the commonwealth of nations, it had preferred consistently to withdraw behind tariff walls and neutrality legislation. God's judgment, however, was not merely a punishment. Niebuhr insisted that God's purpose was always "reconstructive." God's judgment would in fact serve to cleanse societies, stimulate rebuilding, and open a more productive future for the world. "To recognize God at work in the war," as Niebuhr put it, was to "live and act with faith in resurrection."[17]

---

[15]HRN, "The Reformers' Ideal of the Church in the World," address to the Western Section of the World Alliance of Presbyterian Churches, in 1939, Albany, New York, HRN Papers, Harvard Divinity School.

[16]HRN, "War as the Judgment of God," *Christian Century* 59 (13 May 1942): 630-33; "Is God in the War?" ibid. (5 August 1942): 953-55; "War as Crucifixion," ibid. 60 (28 April 1943): 513-15.

[17]HRN, "War as the Judgment of God," 630-33.

Niebuhr also suggested that World War II was analogous to the death of Jesus Christ on the cross. He pointed out that those who had suffered the most were not the ones who had caused the war. The thousands who had died in Czechoslovakia, Norway, the Netherlands, Belgium, Greece, China, and the Phillipines were "innocent victims" who proved that God's justice could only be "vicarious" in its method. No less than at Christ's crucifixion, God was using their suffering to chasten and to change those who were truly guilty.[18] Niebuhr agreed that war did not make for "moral indifference." It underscored the moral earnestness of God and confronted humanity with the tragic consequences of its sins. Yet like the cross of Christ, war for him exploded all retributive theories of justice. In his eyes, there was no "just war." In fact, the suffering and death of its innocent victims served to repudiate every human effort to assess the goodness of self and others and to reward or punish accordingly. In fact, all that humanity might truly hope and rely on in any war was the continued outpouring of the grace of God.[19]

The view of history that served to bolster this perspective on war becomes apparent in *The Meaning of Revelation,* which was published in 1941. In this book Niebuhr squarely confronted the obstacles to faith raised repeatedly for well over a century by empirical methods of analysis. Modern Christians, he wrote, must accept "historical relativism." Their Bible was not only divine revelation, but a collection of historically conditioned statements that could not be interpreted apart from a particular cultural setting. "We live in history," he pointed out, "as the fish is in water and what we mean by the revelation of God can be indicated only as we point through the medium in which we live." He also knew that once such relativity was accepted, "revelation" lost much of its unique authority. The birth of Jesus, the miracles, the parables, the crucifixion and resurrection stories, even the institution of the sacraments, could be explained by noting their place in Jewish or Hellenistic life and thought. In the minds of Christians, Niebuhr emphasized, this approach always seemed to produce doubt rather than certainty. The question remained, "How can revelation mean both history and God?"[20]

Niebuhr's answer was to distinguish "internal" from "external" history. The latter was "objective," he wrote, because it was the point of view of one who stood "outside" the context of events. But it was "impersonal." According to Niebuhr, "external" history focused on ideas, interests, and movements, dividing them into "primary" and "secondary" elements, and furnishing knowledge

---

[18]Ibid., 631.

[19]HRN, "War as Crucifixion," 513-15.

[20]HRN, *The Meaning of Revelation* (New York, 1941) 32-43.

that was descriptive in character. "Internal" historical knowledge, however, was more normative in character. While it sought to remain unbiased, it solicited such valuative responses as love, praise, or anger. Internalists also looked upon society not as individuals joined together by the external bonds of custom, law, and geography, but as a community in which other selves "live in us and we in them." In Niebuhr's terms, "When there is strife in this community there is strife and pain in us and when it is at peace we have peace in ourselves."[21]

Most importantly for Niebuhr, "internal" history furnished a context in which "revelation" meant both "God" and "history." Given its focus on community values, it implied faith in some supreme value. As in any community, its purpose was in fact to mold past and present into forms that prompted devotion to this value.[22] Revelation performed the same role within the Christian community. It furnished the pattern by which Christians interpreted all events, and it called forth allegiance to the one Jesus called "Father." For Niebuhr Jesus was a real person who had lived and died in the first century. But in the "internal" view, what he revealed of God was a "moving thing," the meaning of which could be fully realized only by bringing it to bear on ever new situations and interpreting them as part of a single drama of divine and human interaction.[23]

At no point did Niebuhr mean to suggest that Christianity possessed the only authentic view of history. Judaism, Islam, or another world religion was just as capable of offering an "internal" perspective. He felt Christianity could only "confess" to the world what its revelation permitted it to reconstruct as history.[24] He also stressed that Christians must subject their interpretations of events to "external" historical criticism, lest revelation supplant God as the center of its attention and the ground of its faith.[25]

"Religious objectivist" was the term Niebuhr used to identify himself in answer to critics of his article, "War as the Judgment of God." By this he did not mean to claim that he was able to assume "God's point of view" or that his interpretation of the war was in some sense "divine." Rather, the term described the perspective of one who was persuaded that "divine reason" was involved in all of life and who was thus inclined to look at every particular event as an opportunity to serve God.[26]

---

[21]Ibid., 45-52.

[22]Ibid., 56-59.

[23]Ibid., 97-100.

[24]Ibid., 53-54.

[25]Ibid., 62-63.

[26]HRN, "Is God in the War?" 954.

One of the chief contentions of Niebuhr's critics is that such a view of God at work in history tends to sanction passivity on the part of the church. But does it? Niebuhr himself felt it inspired a stronger sense of moral responsibility. "Conversion" was the label he used to describe the process. "Through Christ," he wrote, "we become immigrants into the empire of God which extends over all the world and learn to remember the history of that empire, that is of men in all times and places, as our history." Clearly, this implied both "repentance" of all efforts to exclude one's own past from that of others and "appropriation" of their faults as one's own sins. For Niebuhr this was the only way for groups to transcend beliefs or images that kept fueling their antagonisms and to move toward reconciliation.[27]

Transformation of America's foreign policy was clearly the aim of Niebuhr's interpretation of World War II. In an article published in 1943, for instance, he asserted that faith in God provoked "permanent revolution" of mind and heart, consistently exposing the relativity of all other values, removing the taboos surrounding those considered too holy for critical inquiry, including democracy, and, in view of the One who had in fact reconciled all of existence, attaching "new sacredness" to enemies.[28] Similarly, in "War as the Judgment of God," Niebuhr insisted that while democratic neighbors might appear to be more worthy of aid, acceptance of God's judgment must bring America to the side of any country in distress, even antidemocratic regimes. America, he urged, must repudiate policies based on "self-defense" or "national interest." It must continue to fight the war until such a time as the interests of weaker nations were as protected as its own and a just and durable peace was insured for all the world.[29]

At the same time, Niebuhr was moving to repudiate other views of the church's role in American politics. In his assessments of World War II he did not complain that pastors and their congregations had repeated the errors for which they had been so severely criticized after 1918. Most seemed to restrain their patriotism and to accent the judgment of God on all nations. But very few, as he saw it, were allowing their understanding of God's judgment to shape their perspective on the fighting itself. Pacifists limited their attention to peacemaking on the grounds that humankind rather than God made war. Nationalists, while stressing that they did not engage in war as Christians, stated that they were obligated to do so as citizens of their country. In Niebuhr's estimation, both groups had compromised the monotheism of the Christian faith.

---

[27]HRN, *The Meaning of Revelation,* 80-88.

[28]HRN, "The Nature and Existence of God: A Protestant View," *Motive* 4 (December 1943): 46.

[29]HRN, "War as the Judgment of God," 632.

The "judge" and "redeemer" of a world at war, he argued, was the "one and universal God," the "Father of all things," not merely a "lord of the spiritual life." Efforts to justify war by separating one's religion from politically expedient action either excluded some part of life from the "reign of God" or else led to the abandonment of monotheism in favor of a "double standard" and a "double deity."[30]

Niebuhr saw this "dualist" fallacy in still another group, which he called the "pragmatists." They were Christians who thought that war required a "double response," one of "contrition" for the sins of fighting and killing, and another of "confident assertion" that democracies like the United States were at least relatively right in opposing totalitarianism. On at least one occasion, Niebuhr called them "ditheists" because they worshiped two gods, the Father of Jesus Christ and their country. Democracy and peace, he agreed, were principles of a high order, as long as they were kept "under God"; but the status to which the "pragmatists" had elevated them made them "rivals" of God that were bound to become "betrayers of life."[31]

Dualists also seemed to distort the biblical perspective on evil. War was no less a human tragedy for Niebuhr than it was for anyone else. Yet he refused to consign it to irrationality or to interpret it as an amoral power struggle in which the fittest survived. To him, such thinking not only contradicted God's sovereignty, but diminished the "good" behavior of many participants in war. Soldiers, for instance, fought not simply for their own interests, but were capable of making sacrifices in behalf of their comrades in arms, for distant values like freedom, or for a new world for their children.[32]

These criticisms of dualism again reveal the contrasts between the approaches of the Niebuhr brothers. World War II did not rekindle the debate in which Richard and Reinhold had become embroiled in 1932. Richard continued to express deep affection and high regard for his brother's influence as a religious leader and editor of *Christianity and Crisis*.[33] Yet the two sharply disagreed when it came to establishing the rationale for America's participation in the war. Joining the "Union for Democratic Action," a group formed in 1941 by liberal former pacifists for the purpose of encouraging an interventionist course of action, Reinhold stressed the difference between "private" and "public" morality and sought to arrive at "approximate" rather than "absolute"

---

[30]Ibid., 631-32.

[31]Ibid., 631.

[32]See HRN, "War as Crucifixion," 513.

[33]HRN to Reinhold Niebuhr, n.d., Reinhold Niebuhr Papers, Library of Congress, Washington DC.

answers for halting totalitarian aggression.[34] For Richard, on the other hand, "absolutes" could not be so compromised, only broken. While he did not ignore the hard realities of war, he refused to restrict God to the spiritual portion of human experience or to invoke the devil in order to save the world. He stubbornly resisted the notion that self-interest and conflict governed all human relationships and preferred to declare his trust in a "goodness" that was using war to reshape humankind's loyalty to the God to whom everything owed its existence.[35]

Their views of history remained the more fundamental bone of contention. The flaw Richard continued to perceive in his brother's approach was not that Reinhold deprived God of a role in history, but that he expected real judgment and redemption to occur only "beyond" history. God remained more "hidden" than revealed in Reinhold's framework, and he seemed to view history as no more than an "interim" between Christ's first and final comings.[36] At one point, Richard went so far as to identify himself with millenarianism because this brand of Christianity clearly anticipated the eternal fulfillment of history in the "here and now." Its perversion, he conceded, was to regard the "partial" as "perfect" fulfillment. Yet it was a view that avoided the traditionalist error of focusing too exclusively on the "eternal," and it refused to allow the world of sin to compromise the principles set forth by the Christian faith.[37] Richard, or so it now appears, was at this point well on his way toward the "radical monotheism" with which he would become identified in the 1950s. During World War II at least, he was already making the "radical" proposal that no event was accidental or meaningless, and that faith was not "monotheistic" unless it embraced the totality of nature and history.[38]

Further refinements in Niebuhr's position became apparent in *Christ and Culture,* published in 1951. The book not only organized the rudiments of Luther and Calvin's approach to church and world into three distinct families, which Niebuhr named synthesist, dualist, and conversionist, but he included in his analysis the teachings of the author of the Gospel of John, St. Paul,

---

[34]See Reinhold Niebuhr, *The Children of Light and the Children of Darkness* (New York, 1944).

[35]HRN, "A Strange Gift . . . and Full of Power," *The Messenger* 9 (25 July 1944): 15.

[36]HRN, "Reinhold Niebuhr's Interpretation of History," paper delivered in 1949 and shared with author by Professor Waldo Beach, Duke Divinity School.

[37]HRN, "Reflections on the Christian Theory of History," paper written for the Theological Discussion Group, n.d., HRN Papers, Yale Divinity School, New Haven CT.

[38]Compare HRN, "Threat and Promise in our Crisis," essay delivered in the context of World War II, HRN Papers, Harvard Divinity School, with *Radical Monotheism and Western Culture* (New York, 1960) 47-48.

Augustine, Thomas Aquinas, and F. D. Maurice. All of them, Niebuhr contended, were determined to deal with church-world problems in "both-and" rather than "either-or" terms. All believed that worldly corruption and wickedness were symptoms of every human being's fall from faith in God. All showed an awareness of the extent to which this disease infected every phase of life, including the church. All sought to combat it at the social as well as the individual level and relied solely on the grace of God for a saving cure. All refused to regard culture as beyond the pale of redemption because Jesus Christ, in their eyes at least, remained the Son of God, its Creator.[39]

"Dualism," however, was clearly a deficiency Niebuhr saw in one of these church-world types. In *Christ and Culture,* he labeled this approach "paradoxical." Paul, Marcion, and especially Luther, he contended, had given too much emphasis to the "sordidness" of everything creaturely. Among these "dualists," as he also referred to them here, creation and the fall were moved into "very close proximity," finiteness was equated with sin, and the transformation of culture was ruled out this side of the grave. In the case of Marcion, such thinking gave rise to an actual "ditheism" in which the God of Jesus Christ was depicted as the rescuer of human souls from the world of evil matter to which a malevolent Creator had attached them. Among Lutheran Protestants, it inspired a division of the world into two kingdoms, set up a separate standard of morality for each, and served to reinforce the cultural conservatism of all who took up their banner. Lutheran churches might call upon princes and citizens, slaves and masters, merchants and consumers, to conform their conduct to the Christian faith. Yet, as Niebuhr saw it, "these were to be improvements within an essentially unchanged context of social habit."[40]

Perhaps the most lucid exposition of Niebuhr's own view appeared in "The Responsibility of the Church for Society." In the article, which became the chapter of a book edited by his Yale colleague, Kenneth Scott Latourette, Niebuhr stated that the scope of the church's obligations to the world was as universal as the God to whom it gave allegiance. The church could neither isolate itself nor ignore any of its neighbors. But how could it avoid becoming "of" the world? Niebuhr outlined the threefold function he now envisioned for the church in the world. As the "apostolic" church it was responsible for proclaiming to every society that God was the center of life and calling for repentance of its idolatries. Yet at the same time Christ compelled the church to assume a "pastoral" role, to participate, that is, in the relief of human need and to alleviate the suffering brought on by injustice. Perhaps the most startling function, however, was his emphasis on the "pioneering" role of the church. Niebuhr

---

[39]HRN, *Christ and Culture* (New York, 1951) 116-20.

[40]Ibid., 149-89.

urged it to become that "element in each particular society" that took the lead in obeying God "on behalf of all." In the work of overcoming the nationalism, racism, and economic imperialism of the world, he asserted, the church must first "repudiate these attitudes within itself."[41]

"Christ the transformer of culture" is the term that best expresses Niebuhr's approach to the world. In this last of the church-world types he discussed in *Christ and Culture* he perceived no fundamental flaw. Especially attractive to him was the balance it struck between God's work as creator and redeemer. Here sin was attributed to the corruption of created goodness rather than creatureliness, and salvation was set forth as a turning of self to God as the true center of life rather than deliverance from the flesh. This approach, he also felt, affirmed the "present" possibility of such renewal. In the mind of Augustine and all others who shared a similar vision of Christ, there was no interim period between the giving of a divine promise and its fulfillment in eternity. World history formed a single drama in which God's determination to redeem the whole creation was consistently being unfolded, and, as it did for Augustine, "conversion" defined the problem of the "world" as well as the purpose of the "church."[42]

3

For Niebuhr, the Cold War years of confrontation with Communism brought the world's problem into sharper relief. In 1944, with the tide of war turning in favor of the Allies, he voiced the hope that neoorthodoxy's emphasis on the transcendent origins of human values might keep Western nations like the United States from developing postwar plans for reconstruction on the basis of self-interest.[43] But in the years that followed he soon discovered that Christianity was being marshaled for the defense of America and the free world. This approach, as Niebuhr saw it in 1946, was a "utilitarian" perversion of religion. It not only suggested that America would have peace as long as it was willing to lay hold of Christianity's spiritual resources, but promised that once the relationship was demonstrated, more of its people would turn to the churches. He warned that however appealing such thinking might be to cultures threatened by enemies and to churches seeking to authenticate faith with tangible results, neither history nor the Bible substantiated it. In fact, some biblical passages seemed to contradict it.[44]

---

[41]HRN, "The Responsibility of the Church for Society," in *The Gospel, the Church, and the World,* ed. Kenneth Scott Latourette (New York, 1946) 111-33.

[42]HRN, *Christ and Culture,* 190-229.

[43]HRN, "Towards a New Otherworldliness," *Theology Today* 1 (April 1944): 78-87.

[44]HRN, "Utilitarian Christianity," *Christianity and Crisis* 6 (8 July 1946): 3-5.

The mass hysteria provoked by McCarthyism tended to compound this problem. Billy Graham's typical altar call put the matter in the most direct terms: "If you would be a true patriot, then become a Christian. If you would be a loyal American, then become a loyal Christian."[45] Similar pressures were applied to promote the cause of Christian unity. A typical argument suggested that churches needed to overcome their differences and pull together in order to strengthen resistance to the Communist foe.[46]

Niebuhr's position was that the real object of America's fears was not Communism but the disintegration of its own society. In an article in 1950 he went so far as to invoke Oswald Spengler's doctrine of dying civilizations and suggested that Americans were turning to religion "with the idea that once upon a time this world was in a much happier state than it is now, that a fall from joy and order has taken place, that this fall was connected with the abandonment of the religion of the fathers, and that if the religion can only be reestablished all may yet be well."[47] Niebuhr believed these fears were combining to make democracy into a new spiritual force; the "American way of life" was becoming a religion. Christianity, on the other hand, demanded obedience to God and called forth repentance not because Americans or their culture might perish if they did not repent, but because, as he put it, "others are now perishing for us" and "we are attacking the very son of God or God himself in our endeavor to escape suffering or to maintain our civilization at any cost." Christianity also condemned the use of atomic weapons not because they might imperil America's future, but because "we have violated our own principles."[48]

So consistently did Niebuhr hold to this conviction that at one point he took issue with those who tried to make "civil rights" part of the prescription for a strong America. He himself opposed racial injustice and regularly incorporated his reasons in his courses on Christian ethics at Yale.[49] Yet Jesus, he told an audience at Howard University, did not preach an "ethics of survival." Rather his was a radical call to belief in the presence of God in all events, one that trusted God's promise of redemption, regardless of whether "civil rights" actually strengthened America's position in the world. It challenged any group

---

[45]Quoted in Winthrop S. Hudson, *Religion in America,* 3d ed. (New York, 1965) 387.

[46]See Samuel McCrea Cavert, *On the Road to Christian Unity: An Appraisal of the Ecumenical Movement* (New York, 1961) 24-25.

[47]HRN, "Evangelical and Protestant Ethics," in *The Heritage of the Reformation,* ed. Elmer J. F. Arndt (New York, 1950) 215-16.

[48]HRN, "Utilitarian Christianity," 5.

[49]See Waldo Beach, "A Theological Analysis of Race Relations," in *Faith and Ethics: The Theology of H. Richard Niebuhr,* ed. Paul Ramsey (New York, 1957) 205-24.

to risk its future and to "live a short time" in loyalty to God and obedience to God's commandment.[50]

Niebuhr also sought to transform Americans' Cold War attitudes toward their enemies. He took strong exception to the prevailing view that the Soviet Union was the epitome of "evil" and the United States of the "good." Both sides of this notion, he thought, contained "illusions," because God's purposes transcended those of any particular nation. The God who sent Assyria to recall Israel to covenant promises of the Old Testament was now using the threat of Communism to pressure America into correcting the racist policies that had marred its own covenant of equality from the beginning, the neglect its special mission to humankind had suffered, and the deep animosity it felt in recent years toward nations like Germany and Japan. Niebuhr did not believe that this perspective made the intentions of the Soviet Union any less destructive. Nor did he call for any abandonment of America's defense. Yet he was firmly convinced that it compelled the American people to embrace the "new values, larger outlook, and deeper understanding" to which God was directing them through an enemy they thought to be evil.[51]

In retrospect Niebuhr's emphasis on democracy's spiritual essence seems to have anticipated Robert Bellah's now famous essay, "Civil Religion in America."[52] The term, of course, was one that Niebuhr never used. Nor did he assign any significant role to Enlightenment religion in the shaping of democratic political thought. Niebuhr's tendency was to ignore the obvious parallels between the Enlightenment's strong sense of the infinite character of Nature's God and Christianity's emphasis on divine sovereignty. He preferred to view Thomas Jefferson, Thomas Paine, and Benjamin Franklin as deistic exponents of the false faith of humanism. The democracy that had marched under the banner of "Republican Religion," he argued in *The Kingdom of God,* was not to be confused with Puritan, separatist, and Quaker thinking, because the dynamic behind it was the "popular" rather than the "divine" will. Besides, the ideal of liberty flowing from the kingdom of Christ was not synonymous with the liberty defined in such Enlightenment documents as the Declaration of Independence. To be sure, the evangelical revivalists had joined forces with the humanist democrats in the fight against the old order. But at no time did they overlook the fallacies inherent in the dogmas of natural liberty and human goodness. The basis of liberty, as they conceived of it, was not the self-evident

---

[50]HRN, *The Gospel for a Time of Fears* (Washington DC, 1950) 10-12, 15-16.

[51]HRN, "The Illusions of Power," *Pulpit* 33 (April 1962): 100-103.

[52]Robert N. Bellah, "Civil Religion in America," *Daedalus* 91 (Winter 1967): 1-21.

rights of humankind, but the conversion of sinners to God.[53] Yet, like Bellah, Niebuhr insisted that America's true allegiance was to the transcendent values on which the founders had first grounded the republic. The function of this "faith," moreover, was "conversion." It was to help America evaluate its policies in such a way that the process of national renewal would never cease.

To help Americans recover this same God-centered perspective on their own ideals and values was one of Niebuhr's chief aims throughout the Cold War era. In his estimation the orientation of liberal historians remained too humanistic. It stereotyped colonial Protestant theology as antidemocratic and falsely linked it with repressive, aristocratic brands of political conservatism, while asserting that belief in human goodness had inspired love for liberty. How then, Niebuhr asked, could a reactionary Calvinist like Jonathan Edwards offer so much intellectual inspiration to America's drive for independence? Or, why did the evangelical sects of the Second Great Awakening give such strong support to the Jacksonian revolution? The time had come, in Niebuhr's view at least, to turn back from the path Parrington had blazed and to consider the antipathy to absolutism that the Protestant doctrines of the sovereignty of God and original sin had instilled in the American mind. These doctrines, he declared, had bolstered the constitutional impulse to limit the power of government and sustained the popular determination to protect the freedom of individuals by the adoption of the Bill of Rights.[54]

There is also an obvious kinship between Niebuhr's position and the view Will Herberg articulated at the midpoint of the 1950s in *Protestant-Catholic-Jew.*[55] Like Herberg, Niebuhr believed that the new religion that the Communist threat helped to nurture focused on the "American way of life." Especially in the lectures that formed the basis of *Radical Monotheism and Western Culture,* he called the American faith of the 1950s a form of nationalism and depicted it as the greatest threat to the theological foundations on which America's constitutional government rested. He stressed that it was really a type of henotheism, a rival of genuine faith in God, because it relied on the nation to supply and protect life. The battle between monotheist and henotheist faiths, he also emphasized, took place at every point in the democratic process. It broke out whenever politicians made the "voice of the people" the first

---

[53]HRN, *Kingdom of God in America,* 124.

[54]Niebuhr developed this point most fully in a lecture at Princeton University, "The Idea of Original Sin in American Culture," 24 February 1949, HRN Papers, Harvard Divinity School.

[55]Will Herberg, *Protestant-Catholic-Jew: An Essay in American Religious Sociology* (Garden City NY, 1955). Herberg's analysis of "Protestantism" seems to have relied heavily on Niebuhr; twenty of the first 37 reference notes to this sixth chapter give credit to *Social Sources of Denominationalism.*

and last word in enacting legislation. Those who lived by faith in God were bound to assert that no popular majority could arrogate absolute authority to itself. They acknowledged the relativity of all human judgments, even as they kept striving to make decisions that would conform to the universal context their faith had staked out. Finally, for them, the principle of religious liberty implied that loyalty to God and responsibility as a member of the universal commonwealth of humankind took precedence over any obligations one might owe to the state.[56]

All in all, the crisis of World War II helped to bring about an important set of refinements in Niebuhr's perspective on church and world. Participation in the heated debate between isolationists and interventionists diminished the plausibility of his earlier strategy of "withdrawal" and called forth an approach that clearly exposed the nationalist aspects of the conflict without committing the church to the politics of war or peace. The severe test that war itself posed to his monotheistic outlook served to direct his thinking along a "conversionist" rather than a "dualist" or "synthesist" path. In his view, proponents of the "synthesist" option also combined appreciation of culture with loyalty to Christ and shared Christ's desire to work for the transformation of every aspect of the world. Yet their tendency was to identify Christ with the church and to ignore the evil at work in their own best efforts. The weakness was one that Niebuhr perceived as much in contemporary Christianity as he did in the medieval theology of Thomas Aquinas.

---

[56]HRN, *Radical Monotheism and Western Culture,* 64-77.

Dr. Richard Niebuhr
(Alfred Eisenstaedt, *Life Magazine,* © 1955 Time Inc.)

CHAPTER IV

Continuing the Church's Reformation

"My primary concern today . . . is still that of the reformation of the church. I still believe that reformation is a permanent movement, that metanoia *is the continuous demand made on us in historical life."*

H. Richard Niebuhr
"Reformation: Continuing Imperative," 250

Richard Niebuhr's vocational commitment to the church seldom failed to impress colleagues and students at Yale Divinity School. Even if the subject was one he had addressed on many occasions, his lectures were always carefully prepared and delivered with the gestures of a person endeavoring to feel what he was thinking and to give birth to a more relevant set of insights. "Nobody asks questions in Niebuhr's *Christian Ethics,*" a student is said to have written to a classmate. "That would be like shouting in a cathedral."[1] Apparent as well was the warm, evangelical spirit that Niebuhr's family had modeled for him. During the 1950s he defended the intellectual activity of schools like Yale, calling it a legitimate way for the church to exercise love of God and neighbor. But at the same time he warned that by itself, such activity might reduce God to an abstraction and limit the development of students to their "studious, mental self." While the ministry in his estimation was not restricted to fully mature Christians, it did require that "something of the mind of Christ" be found in candidates for the office and that all such persons be at least "growing toward maturity." So he also stressed the importance of such "other activities"

[1]Quoted in Liston Pope, "H. Richard Niebuhr: A Personal Appreciation," in *Faith and Ethics: The Theology of H. Richard Niebuhr,* ed. Paul Ramsey (New York, 1957) 5.

in the program of the divinity school as field work duties, and he urged both students and faculty to participate in chapel services.[2]

With devotion, however, Niebuhr consistently mixed healthy doses of criticism of the church. To see this, one has only to examine a sampling of the writings he published following World War II. In 1951, for example, he argued that the genuine intentions motivating so many foreign missionaries were warped by feelings of white superiority and the identification of Christianity with Western beliefs and values. Redemption, as he saw it, involved a repentance that made restitution for these past sins and a redirection of mission work by the spirit of Christ.[3] More extensive comments came to light in the Montgomery Lectures of 1957 that were eventually published as part of *Radical Monotheism and Western Culture.* Here Niebuhr maintained that "monotheism" was not simply a type of faith, but a principle that served to further religious revitalization. It kept checking those who tried to invest sacred trust in the symbols of their religion, to so identify themselves with their own group that reverence for these and faith in God became identical.[4] Perhaps his most explicit statement appeared in his contribution to the *Christian Century*'s "How My Mind Has Changed" series of 1960. "I see our religion now," he wrote, "as one part of our human culture which like other parts is subject to a constant process of reformation and deformation, of *metanoia* (repentance) and fall." He went on to state that if his "Protestantism" had motivated him in the past to "protest" against the spirit of capitalism, nationalism, Communism, and technological civilization, it now led him to "protest" the "deification" of Scriptures and the church.[5]

In Niebuhr's view, there were ways in which the "church" clearly resembled the "world." Its traditions and rituals were often no less flawed by human sinfulness than other aspects of culture. Self-serving motives distorted Christian prayers, and self-righteousness diluted the church's witness to non-Christian cultures. Worst of all, the churches could be as guilty of substituting some little god for the One beyond the many. As he saw it, God demanded that the

---

[2]See H. Richard Niebuhr (hereafter cited as HRN), *The Purpose of the Church and Its Ministry: Reflections on the Aims of Theological Education* (New York, 1956) 107-34; H. Richard Niebuhr, Daniel Day Williams, and James M. Gustafson, "The Main Issues in Theological Education," *Theology Today* 11 (January 1955): 518.

[3]HRN, "An Attempt at a Theological Analysis of Missionary Motivation," *Occasional Bulletin* 14 (January 1963): 1-6. Niebuhr first prepared this paper for the Division of Foreign Missions of the National Council of Churches in April 1951.

[4]HRN, *Radical Monotheism and Western Culture* (New York, 1960) 49-63.

[5]HRN, "Reformation: Continuing Imperative," *Christian Century* 77 (2 March 1960): 259.

church undergo the same process of conversion from idolatry to faith to which it called society and individuals.

1

Niebuhr's greatest concern appears to have been the temper of contemporary religious life. Following World War II, both Protestantism and Catholicism in America were experiencing unparalleled growth; at almost every level of their institutions there was evidence of a "return to religion." Church membership increased from 49 percent of the total population in 1940 to 55 percent in 1950 and to 69 percent by 1960. When asked by the Census Bureau in 1957 to identify their "religion," 96 percent of the American people cited a specific affiliation. Church attendance surged. Released from the restrictions depression and war had imposed, church investments in new construction leaped from $76 million in 1946 to $775 million in 1956, and by 1960 topped the billion-dollar mark.[6]

During few other periods in America's history did religion gain as much public recognition. Popular religious books were read as never before, and leaders like Billy Graham, Norman Vincent Peale, and Bishop Fulton J. Sheen gained national attention through the press and television. The phrase "under God" was added to the pledge of allegiance, and "In God We Trust" became the official motto stamped on America's currency. Attitudes toward neoorthodox theologians also shifted to the positive; Reinhold Niebuhr and Paul Tillich in particular were touted for the respect they had gained among secular intellectuals.[7]

Astounding as well were developments associated with the ecumenical movement. The formation of the World Council of Churches at Amsterdam in 1948 and a subsequent assembly of this same group at Evanston, Illinois, in 1954 helped sharpen the desire for unity among American Protestants. In 1950 eight interdenominational agencies, including the older Federal Council of Churches, merged to form the National Council of Churches. Among the more significant church unions were the creation of the United Church of Christ in 1957 and the mergers of several German and Scandinavian families of Lutherans into the American Lutheran Church in 1960 and the Lutheran Church in America in 1962.[8]

Yet in all of this religious ferment, Richard Niebuhr saw few signs of real renewal. One aspect of it that he found especially disturbing was the fusion of

---

[6]Sydney E. Ahlstrom, *A Religious History of the American People* (New Haven, 1972) 952-53.

[7]Winthrop S. Hudson, *Religion in America,* 3d ed. (New York, 1965) 384-88.

[8]H. Shelton Smith, Robert T. Handy, and Lefferts A. Loetscher, eds., *American Christianity,* 2 vols. (New York, 1963) 2: 563-74.

Christianity with the "American way of life." To him, church attendance had become a way of avoiding suspicion of being a subversive influence; it attested not to a revival of faith in God, but to the "survival" ethic of a nation locked into a Cold War with the Soviet Union and its Communist allies.[9] Other features of the revival were just as troubling to Niebuhr. He perceived widespread dissatisfaction with churches on the part of faithful members and nominal Christians alike, among clergy as well as laity. The rate of "Christian illiteracy," he also claimed, remained far too high. Great numbers of Protestants scarcely seemed to understand that the Christian faith taught something specific about God, and that it involved not simply a code of ethics, but an orientation toward all of life.[10] In 1960 Niebuhr looked back on the revival more as an awakening of a "desire for faith" than as a renewal of real faith in God. More people, to be sure, were asking religious questions about themselves and the world. Yet for too many, the traditional answers offered by the church seemed hollow. Others were choosing to remain alienated from the church. Especially haunting to Niebuhr was the phrase: "The hungry sheep look up and are not fed."[11]

Some of Niebuhr's sharpest criticisms were directed at the fundamentalist elements among the growing number of American Protestants. Their approach to the world, as he saw it, fit the Christ-of-culture mold and showed that their battle against liberalism was in fact a "family quarrel." To him, the logic of both groups was remarkably similar. Both identified Christ with "what men conceive to be their finest ideals, their noblest institutions, and their best philosophy." Among fundamentalists, however, the "culture" was nineteenth-century America. For them, obedience to Christ meant prohibition of such practices as drinking and dancing, and, given their older view of earth's creation, opposition to modern science.[12]

Niebuhr linked this deficiency with fundamentalist views of biblical authority, which he regarded as idolatrous because they tended to make the Bible rather than God the object of Christian devotion. For himself, Niebuhr considered the Bible an indispensable resource, without which the Christian community could not carry on its work. In his article "The Norm of the Church," for example, he emphasized both the "corroborative" and the "educational" na-

---

[9]See HRN, *The Gospel for a Time of Fears* (Washington DC, 1950).

[10]HRN, "Who are the Unbelievers and What Do They Believe?" Report submitted to the Secretariat for Evangelism, World Council of Churches, in *The Christian Hope and the Task of the Church: Six Ecumenical Surveys and the Report of the Assembly Prepared by the Advisory Commission on the Main Theme, 1954* (New York, 1954) 35-37.

[11]HRN, "Reformation: Continuing Imperative," 250-51.

[12]See HRN, *Christ and Culture* (New York, 1951) 102-103.

ture of biblical authority. Though he did not use either term at the time,[13] he stated that for Christians the Bible functioned as a "consistent and unchanging objective criterion" that continually enabled the church to eliminate aberrations and to validate its true purposes. It also taught Christians how to live before God in the world by exposing them to the "mind of Christ."[14] Yet biblicism, as he saw it, denied both the "final claim of God" and the "content of the scriptures themselves." Because its tendency was to restrict revelation to "records of the past," it failed to see the Bible as a "dictionary" for interpreting whatever a "living God" was "doing" and "declaring" at any given moment in the experience of humankind.[15]

Niebuhr perceived a similar malady at work in the neoorthodox movement of this period. As early as 1944 he voiced concern over the approach of some of its exponents, especially those who either came across as too polemical or else tried to repristinate the Christian faith. The tendency of the latter, he argued, was to emphasize "tradition" rather than the reality to which it pointed and to churn up much "fruitless quarrel" among interpreters of the classics in Christian doctrine.[16] This aspect of neoorthodoxy was for him the "monstrous illusion" of which Søren Kierkegaard had sought to warn the church. It implied that the church and its teachings were "objective." Christians, he stressed in 1956, must follow Kierkegaard's advice and always direct attention "away from themselves to the eternal, to Christ, to the ultimate, to the absolute."[17]

Similar criticisms surfaced in Niebuhr's assessments of Karl Barth's influence. He felt that Barth's inclination was to look upon faith as "assent" or "right believing" and to give renewed emphasis to orthodoxy as "right teaching" and "right doctrine."[18] Niebuhr agreed that "expressions of faith" were important, because they brought one into dialogue with other interpreters of Christianity. Yet the conversation was never a process of simply repeating the ideas of others. It forced one to look beyond them, to confront the actual divine and human realities to which they pointed, and to solicit their aid in examining one's

---

[13]The terms are used in James M. Gustafson's introduction to HRN, *The Responsible Self* (New York, 1963) 19-25.

[14]HRN, "The Norm of the Church," *Journal of Religious Thought* 4 (Autumn-Winter 1946-1947) 11-12.

[15]HRN, *Purpose of the Church and Its Ministry,* 43-44; "Reformation: Continuing Imperative," 250.

[16]HRN, "Towards a New Other-Worldliness," *Theology Today* 1 (April 1944): 85-87.

[17]HRN, "Søren Kierkegaard," in *Christianity and the Existentialists,* ed. Carl Michalson (New York, 1956) 23-42.

[18]HRN, "Reformation: Continuing Imperative," 250.

own concerns.[19] As contemporary theologians endeavored to interpret older formulations in the modern setting, new light frequently broke forth not because they were giving new answers to old questions, but because they were asking different questions and devising new methods for discerning answers. Niebuhr took the position that if neoorthodoxy were truly to "recover" Christianity's traditional elements, it must consistently subject them to new inquiry and new interpretation. Then, and only then, would it contribute to the formation of a "living tradition" in theology.[20]

Such concerns served to temper Niebuhr's earlier criticisms of liberal Christianity. During the 1920s and 1930s he had taken strong exception to its heady optimism and unqualified faith in humankind and had called for a return to belief in God as a transcendent reality. Following World War II, however, he pointed out several ironic consequences of nineteenth-century liberal scholarship. Liberals, he maintained, had set out to emancipate Christianity from the fetters of biblical literalism. Yet in adopting the historical-critical method of interpretation, they had in fact awakened a new interest in biblical studies and heightened the church's appreciation of the prophetic and apostolic legacies of faith. Adolf von Harnack's scholarship, as he saw it, had met with similar results. While his aim was to reconstruct Christianity on the basis of present experience, his research into the past had actually deepened the church's awareness of history and broadened its sense of participation in it.[21] Niebuhr continued to consider the Barthian "correction" of liberal Christianity in the 1920s "absolutely essential." Yet by 1960 he labeled it an "over-correction" and began to allude to "new studies in modern theology" that had shown him that the "line of march begun in Schleiermacher's day" was not as "humanistic" as he had once thought.[22]

Another aspect of liberalism that became increasingly appealing to Niebuhr was its commitment to adapting Christianity to the modern outlook. In his view, the postwar revival included too many churchgoers who were obviously seeking to find safety in "old-time religion." Jesus, they were led to believe, was the answer to all of today's problems. But seldom did this faith furnish any real understanding of the steps one might take to resolve them.[23] In ex-

---

[19]See HRN, "The Gift of the Catholic Vision," *Theology Today* 4 (January 1948): 518-20.

[20]HRN, "Living Tradition in Theology," unpublished essay delivered in 1956, HRN Papers, Harvard Divinity School, Cambridge MA.

[21]HRN, "The Gift of the Catholic Vision," 507-509; "The Seminary in the Ecumenical Age," *Theology Today* 17 (October 1960): 303-305.

[22]HRN, "Reformation: Continuing Imperative," 250.

[23]HRN, "The Old-Time Religion Isn't Good Enough," unpublished sermon delivered in 1959, HRN Papers, Harvard Divinity School.

pressing this concern, Niebuhr seemed to be anticipating the "death-of-God" controversy that erupted in the mid-1960s.[24] "Our old phrases are worn out," he declared; "they have become cliches by means of which we can neither grasp nor communicate the reality of our existence before God." He insisted that the Christian message must undergo a complete "resymbolization." This process for him amounted to more than "retranslation," the finding, that is, of a modern vocabulary for such older Christian concepts as "redemption" and "justification." It meant knowledge of the "actualities" to which persons in the past were referring when they employed the terms as well as reinterpretation of their meaning with the aid of contemporary ideas and experience.[25] Among the theologians of the 1950s, Rudolf Bultmann seemed to be making progress along these lines. Niebuhr openly confessed the "great kinship" he had come to feel with Bultmann in his efforts to demythologize the Christian faith and to set forth a new symbolization of it that was coherent with existentialist philosophy.[26]

2

Historically, Niebuhr saw Roman Catholicism as the most culpable Christian group. In *Christ and Culture* he drew attention to medieval efforts to set the church "above" the world and recognized that Thomas Aquinas had demonstrated how Christianity "superadded" demands and promises of God that lay beyond the range of human reason. To him, this effort to blend philosophy and theology satisfied the human desire for unity of superstructure. But later Catholic theologians showed reluctance either to acknowledge the "relative" character of Aquinas's great "synthesis" or to move beyond it. Such popes as Leo XIII tended to identify Christ with the institution and doctrines of the church. This had occurred, Niebuhr argued, because if "synthesis" is viewed "as a purely symbolic action, as a humble, acknowledgedly fallible attempt, as the human side of an action that cannot be completed without the deed of God who also initiated it," it is not really "synthesis." It can in fact only lead to an approach to culture other than the "synthesist."[27] For him, the first major step in this direction was the Protestant Reformation. In *Christ and Culture* he em-

---

[24]"Death of God" theology generally discounted not God, but the idolatry of traditional pictures of God. Thomas J. J. Altizer and William Hamilton (*Radical Theology and the Death of God* [Indianapolis, 1966], Gabriel Vahanian (*The Death of God* [New York, 1961]), Bishop John A. T. Robinson (*Honest to God* [Philadelphia, 1963]), and Harvey Cox (*The Secular City* [New York, 1965]) were among its leading proponents.

[25]HRN, "Reformation: Continuing Imperative," 251.

[26]Ibid., 250.

[27]HRN, *Christ and Culture,* 141-48.

phasized that Martin Luther had rejected the "synthesist solution" because he understood that evil infected "saintliness" as much as it did the ordinary aspects of living.[28]

Here and elsewhere during the postwar era, Niebuhr also sought to emphasize the positive side of this assertion. He contended that the essence of the Reformation was "renewal" of the church's faith. It had forced simple folk and great leaders alike to look beyond the traditional symbols of the church and to wrestle with God directly. Especially for those who had lost confidence in the church or in their own ability to lift themselves to sainthood, it brought forth a "new reliance" on God. Niebuhr dismissed the notion that the Reformation was primarily a rebellion against authority. On the contrary, he argued, it involved both "moral seriousness" about the sorry state of human affairs and "faith" that the promise of salvation applied to the present as much as the future.[29]

At the same time, Niebuhr acknowledged that Protestants had not always exercised sufficient self-criticism. In fact, in 1950 he introduced two conflicting views of the Reformation. The one, which he labeled "Protestant," took a defensive posture. It tended to identify true Christianity with Protestant culture and looked upon the Reformation as a tradition to conserve or use for the purpose of exposing the errors of Roman Catholicism. The "Evangelical" view, which was also Niebuhr's, referred to the "spirit" in which all Christians lived. Niebuhr called it a "movement that always emanated from a direct encounter with God." It demanded that sin be recognized in oneself as well as others. It promoted not fear or heresy hunts, but freedom to respond with the creativity of the gospel to the ever changing circumstances of life in the world.[30]

Niebuhr also called attention to ways Protestant thinking could become as idolatrous as that of Roman Catholicism. Some Protestants, he asserted, chose to orient theology toward the Bible rather than toward the God it revealed. Others confused the authority of religious experience or conscience with the God to whom both bore witness. Just as perverse in his estimation was the "new legalism" that could become rampant among members of both of these groups. Niebuhr in fact argued that the vigorous moral codes authored by such second-generation Puritans as Cotton Mather were more reflective of the constraints of medieval monasticism than the new freedom brought about by the Refor-

---

[28]Ibid., 172.

[29]HRN, "The Protestant Movement and Democracy in the United States," in *Religion in American Life,* vol. 1, *The Shaping of American Religion,* ed. James Ward Smith and A. Leland Jamison (Princeton, 1961) 22-36.

[30]HRN, "Evangelical and Protestant Ethics," in *The Heritage of the Reformation,* ed. Elmer J. F. Arndt (New York, 1950) 211-19.

mation in the areas of sex and family life. "It is only remarkable," he observed, "that Protestantism itself illustrates the prevalence of the human moral orientation which it tends to associate in peculiar fashion with Roman Catholic doctrine and polity; and that it makes evident in its own history and actions man's inconquerable desire to defend and justify himself by his good works as well as to identify his social and personal culture with God's revelation of his will."[31]

Niebuhr's sketch of F. D. Maurice in *Christ and Culture* might be viewed as another illustration. For Niebuhr, this British theologian of the nineteenth century saw the sin of self-centeredness in the Christian Socialists he supported as well as in the commercial capitalists he condemned. He scored religious people in general, particularly those who might confess that they belonged to a "guilty race" but still hoped for a "separate pardon," who sought to justify themselves by faith held as a "possession" or by a "righteousness of their own," who remained connected with parties and sects within the church that pointed to themselves as the way to salvation. Maurice, Niebuhr seemed to think, called for the reform of the "church" as much as the "world." He not only regarded the church's corruption as an "outrage on the Christian principle," but was wise enough to know that even when the goal was to unite people "in Christ," the process usually demanded uniformity in "certain notions about Christ."[32]

In Niebuhr's perspective on the Reformation, we also see a striking parallel with the work of Paul Tillich. In *The Protestant Era* Tillich, like Niebuhr, emphasized the "principle" rather than the "historical reality" of Protestantism's formative era. He insisted that the former represented the prophetic element in the church's voice, directed against all attempts to exalt finite institutions and authorities to the level of the infinite or to treat relative beliefs and traditions, including those of Protestantism itself, as if they were absolute.[33] Niebuhr described his own view as one that perceived in history a rhythmic pattern of "revival" and "protest" against many successive "established orders." For those who assumed it, Christianity became a "movement," a process of "becoming," the story of "many reformations."[34]

At the same time, Niebuhr refused to see "reformation" and concern for the "catholicity" of the church as incompatible Christian objectives. At one point he even called himself a "Protestant Catholic." To insist that the church must "protest" every attempt to identify certain doctrines with divine truth or to claim

---

[31]HRN, "Evangelical and Protestant Ethics," 217-18.

[32]HRN, *Christ and Culture,* 223-24.

[33]See Paul Tillich, *The Protestant Era,* abr. ed. (Chicago, 1948) 192-221.

[34]HRN, "The Protestant Movement and Democracy in the United States," 22-26.

that one of its institutions had authority over the whole church, he pointed out, was actually a more "catholic" outlook than the one set forth in Roman Catholicism. It in fact served to prevent the church from excluding even those elements against whom their "protest" might be lodged.[35] Niebuhr also thought that Reformation theology united Protestants and Catholics as much as it divided them. Its fresh emphasis on the kingdom of God, he argued, compelled each to deal with the other out of "charity" rather than "fear," in terms of the shared experience of God's grace rather than mere tolerance. It furnished a context large enough to help Protestants appreciate the gifts of order and unity Catholicism had bequeathed to the church as a whole and to lead Catholics to recognize that "protest" might serve to stimulate reform of their structures and advance their cause. "If we approach Protestant-Roman Catholic relations in this mood," he exclaimed, "we shall also look forward to the future with the hope that at some time the great division of Christendom will be overcome."[36]

3

Because of his commitment to continuing the church's reformation, in part by healing its greatest division, Niebuhr supported the modern ecumenical movement. He not only lauded the "catholic vision" that ecumenists were helping to revive among Christians in general, but contributed theological essays to the Amsterdam assembly of the World Council of Churches and to its subsequent meeting in Evanston, Illinois.[37] He also recognized the potential advantages of ecumenism's institutional goals and hailed the merger of his own Evangelical and Reformed church with the Congregational Christian churches as a positive step in the direction of Protestant unification.[38] Neoorthodoxy, as he saw it, had strengthened the ecumenical movement. Liberal scholarship, modern science, and the social gospel, to be sure, had contributed to the development of a common Christian mind. Communism had furnished a common foe.[39] Still, it was neoorthodoxy that had recovered the doctrine of the one, universal church. Since the movement continued to address all theology from that standpoint, its outlook was thoroughly ecumenical.

---

[35]HRN, "The Gift of the Catholic Vision," 516-17.

[36]HRN, "Issues Between Catholics and Protestants," *Religion in Life* 23 (Spring 1954): 199-205.

[37]HRN, "The Disorder of Man in the Church of God," in *Man's Disorder and God's Design,* volume 1, *The Universal Church in God's Design* (New York, 1949) 78-88; "Who Are the Unbelievers and What Do They Believe?" 35-37.

[38]HRN, "Another Church Union," *The Messenger* 8 (6 April 1943): 430-31.

[39]HRN, "The Gift of the Catholic Vision," 507-10.

An article Niebuhr published in *Theology Today* in 1946, "The Doctrine of the Trinity and the Unity of the Church," might be viewed as a typical illustration of this feature of neoorthodoxy. He claimed that although all Christians shared a common monotheism, they tended to part company over how God became known and to gravitate toward one of three "unitarian" religions. Unitarians of the Creator rebelled against worshiping the Christ revealed in the New Testament. Those who reacted against preoccupation with natural knowledge of God drifted into a unitarianism of God the Son. Holy Spirit unitarianism developed as a protest against anyone who dared to divorce the knowledge of God from personal experience. This pattern of behavior, Niebuhr argued, contributed to the division of churches. Yet it actually demonstrated the interdependence of Christians. It showed that "truth" was not "the possession of any individual or any party or school," but was represented "only by the dynamic and complementary work of the company of knowers and believers." Those who worshiped only God the Creator might discover that Jesus Christ revealed the merciful and gracious attributes of the Father. Christ unitarians might learn that faith in the Redeemer implied faith in the Creator. And to Spirit unitarians it might be revealed that certainty depended on knowledge of both the Son and the Father.[40]

Despite his commitment to an ecumenical outlook, Niebuhr was clearly uncomfortable with some of the ecumenical aspects of America's "return to religion." Particularly troubling were the antiinstitutional attitudes reflected in the movement itself. He shared many of the sentiments of the *Christian Century*'s editor, Charles Clayton Morrison, who branded denominationalism an anachronism in an age of tolerance and enlightenment; it embarrassed missionaries, frustrated the social gospel, stifled the ministry of pastors and their congregations, and above all kept the one true church of Christ from becoming an empirical reality.[41] Yet Niebuhr refused to attribute Christian disunity and discord to church structures alone. To him, the real problem lay in the disobedience and lack of faith that infected all aspects of the church's behavior. Two of the more obvious instances he chose to cite were the "loveless discipline" that cast out members who dared to follow a different course of conduct and the "loveless lack of discipline" that sacrificed real commitment to Christ for the sake of keeping or adding membership.[42] Reformation, he insisted, always implied internal rebirth under the gospel. The process involved not the creation of new organizations, but the "conversion" of existing ones, a turning

---

[40]HRN, "The Doctrine of the Trinity and the Unity of the Church," *Theology Today* 3 (October 1946): 371-84.

[41]Charles Clayton Morrison, *The Unfinished Reformation* (New York, 1953) 26-73.

[42]HRN, "The Disorder of Man in the Church of God," 78-88.

away, that is, from self to God and a turning of hearts toward each other in reconciliation because of divine forgiveness.[43]

Just as disturbing was the Augustinian distinction between the "visible" and the "invisible" church which neoorthodoxy had revived among ecumenists. Niebuhr thought that the distinction helped to show the difference between the one church of which Christ was the Head and the many organizations Christians had erected. Neoorthodoxy focused almost exclusively on the fact that churches were "contradictory" to the eternal reality of the church. Niebuhr contended, however, that Christians could not "aspire after membership in the Church without joining the churches." Nor could they "build the holy Catholic society, the universal fellowship of reconciliation, without increasing, reforming, supporting, and defending these contradictory organizations—our religious institutions, the Western counterparts of Shintoist and Hindu cults." He insisted that the "visible" and the "invisible" churches belonged together; both were present wherever Christians gathered. The corruptions of "visible" Christianity were apparent in those who belonged to the "invisible" church. Yet elements of the "invisible" also appeared in the "visible." The best perspective on all of this, as he saw it, was eschatological; the "invisible" church was an "emergent" reality within the churches and served, at least in part, to further unity with God and the rest of humankind.[44]

This view represents a significant shift in attitude from Niebuhr's earlier works. In *Social Sources of Denominationalism* Niebuhr had decried the worldly corruption reflected in the church's institutional structures. In *The Kingdom of God* he had intensified his onslaught, arguing that denominations had lost sight of the invisible catholic church, confused themselves with their cause, and identified the kingdom of Christ with their own peculiar doctrines and practice. Aggressive unity, he pointed out, had given way to self-consciousness and competitiveness, both of which corrupted their missionary and educational enterprises.[45]

In the period following World War II, Niebuhr did not repudiate these earlier criticisms of religious denominations. Yet in his postwar lectures and writings he added a new set of observations. The free and highly competitive environment of America, as he now saw it, not only tended to increase the fractionalizing tendencies of Protestant groups, but spawned countervailing movements toward unity. Religious groups that had been divided by political ideology and cultural differences in the Old World or torn apart by schisms in the New

---

[43]HRN, "The Hidden Church and the Churches of Sight," *Religion in Life* 15 (Winter 1945-1946): 115-16.

[44]Ibid., 107-15.

[45]HRN, *The Kingdom of God in America* (New York, 1937) 177-78.

now had the freedom to merge. Christians were able at any time to form voluntary associations for the purpose of achieving common ends. They could work together for peace or temperance. They could meet together as associations, councils, or federations of churches.

In Niebuhr's revised view, competition for membership and support could produce healthy as well as deplorable traits. Actually, this natural rivalry had encouraged the churches to penetrate every phase of American life, to develop programs capable of meeting specific needs, and to articulate their faith in a down-to-earth manner.[46] Niebuhr also contended that no matter how ecumenically minded Christians might become, they remained dependent on their church organizations. "Community" and "institution" were in fact the terms he used to emphasize these "polar characteristics" of the church and to assert that it could neither be "defined" nor "served" without some reference to both.[47]

In Niebuhr's estimation, the ecumenical movement tended to distort the monotheistic faith of Christianity. This he saw as early as the publication of Charles Clayton Morrison's *What Is Christianity?* Morrison's attempt to present the Christian church as the "revelation of God," Niebuhr warned in his review of the book, was "wholly out of line" with the "work of standard theologians of all times." That view, Niebuhr insisted, was morally "dangerous" because it invited the church to become another of the world's "overly self-conscious communities," all of which were prone to make "self-defense" the "first law of life."[48] Even more explicit criticisms of all such views appeared in *Radical Monotheism.* Christians, Niebuhr argued, could so rely on the church for truth and salvation that faith in God became a matter of being converted to the church. Such church-centeredness, however, was in fact a henotheistic form of religion. It not only allowed the church to take the place of God as the object of faith, but sought the unity of the church not as a testimony to the "universal dominion of God," but as a way of calling attention to Christianity's own "true being."[49]

Closely associated with this same perversion, in Niebuhr's estimation, was the almost singular emphasis ecumenists placed on Jesus Christ. For him, the proper Christian perspective on God was trinitarian, involving the Father and the Holy Spirit as well as the Son of God. To take the position that Jesus Christ

---

[46]While a number of unpublished addresses and lectures from the 1950s reveal Niebuhr's "second thoughts" on denominationalism, the best published resource is "The Protestant Movement and Democracy in the United States."

[47]HRN, *Purpose of the Church and Its Ministry,* 21-23.

[48]HRN, review of *What is Christianity?* by Charles Clayton Morrison, *Journal of Religion* 21 (April 1941): 189-92.

[49]HRN, *Radical Monotheism and Western Culture,* 59-60.

created, redeemed, and ruled all things amounted to a new unitarianism, one that differed from the unitarianism that had sprung up during the Enlightenment only in the priority it gave to the second person of the Trinity.[50] Niebuhr recognized that neoorthodoxy, and Barth in particular, had popularized Christomonism among Protestants of the 1950s. Yet this did not keep him from attacking its tendencies to transform theology into Christology and to turn the Christian community into a "Jesus-cult." Worse yet, he maintained, were the effects of this faith on the church's attitude toward the world. Christians who saw themselves as a "special group" with a God and destiny apart from the rest of humanity, wrote Niebuhr, were erecting the very walls Christ had come to break down, and they were denying the "society of universal being" to which he had called them.[51]

4

Opportunity to actually reform the church came in 1954 as Niebuhr took charge of a study of theological education in the United States and Canada. Initiated by the American Association of Theological Schools and funded by the Carnegie Corporation, the project called for an intensive investigation of more than a hundred church seminaries and divinity schools. As director of the project, Niebuhr worked with Daniel Day Williams and James Gustafson to gather views of theological education, definitions of purpose, method, and responsibilities, and suggestions for improvement. Members of the staff visited ninety seminaries and interviewed a number of denominational executives, pastors, and students, as well as representatives of the business, labor, and academic communities. Their findings were made available in three separate publications. In the first, *The Purpose of the Church and Its Ministry,* Niebuhr shared his own reflections on the aims of theological education. In the second, *The Advancement of Theological Education,* Niebuhr, Williams, and Gustafson provided an interpretive summary of the data. In the third, a series of bulletins, attention was given to special problems such as the training of pastors from minority groups. Also published shortly thereafter was *The Ministry in Historical Perspectives,* containing a collection of essays written by prominent church historians and edited by Niebuhr and Williams.[52] According to Gustafson, Niebuhr relished the opportunity the entire project afforded him to ad-

---

[50]HRN, "The Doctrine of the Trinity and the Unity of the Church," 374-76; *Purpose of the Church and Its Ministry,* 44-46.

[51]HRN, *Radical Monotheism and Western Culture,* 59-60.

[52]HRN, *Purpose of the Church and Its Ministry;* HRN with Daniel Day Williams and James M. Gustafson, *The Advancement of Theological Education* (New York, 1957); HRN and Daniel Day Williams, eds. *The Ministry in Historical Perspectives* (New York, 1956).

dress the administration of so many schools and found it exhilarating to review the data collected by the staff.[53]

The rationale Niebuhr gave for the project was "the Christian demand for daily and life-long repentance." In his estimation, this was as applicable to divinity schools as to individuals.[54] Faith in God, he asserted, might make this process "less frenetic." However, reform was bound to lead to "even deeper dissatisfaction" because all improvements in theological education would be seen as finite products of the human enterprise.[55] Uppermost in Niebuhr's mind were the effects of the religious revival of the 1950s on theological education. For instance, he considered it a disservice to students for schools to take the neoorthodox position of Emil Brunner that the institutional church could never become the *ecclesia,* or the New Testament fellowship of Christ. Ministerial preparation, he warned, was always for "particular service" in a "local" congregation, apart from which the one church of Christ did not exist.[56] On the other hand, the overall influence of ecumenism still drew Niebuhr's praise. While the idea of a "universal Church" was seldom expressed directly, he found a sense of participation in it "very pervasive." Signs of Christian unity were unmistakable, especially in school objectives, in the contents of their libraries and courses, and in the establishment of programs that were more and more explicitly interdenominational in character.[57]

Niebuhr's antidote for other neoorthodox perversions of Christianity became prominent in the new "purpose" the project set forth for the church. The "increase among men of the love of God and neighbor," he stressed, always meant devotion to both the "Source and Center of all being" and "all that participates in being," for Augustine among the church fathers no more than Socrates in Athens, the Russian people, and the unborn millions to whom the present generation of humanity was responsible for the administration of the world's resources.[58] Both here and elsewhere in his writings from this period, Niebuhr seemed to be taking the bold step of bringing his "reformation" principle to bear on Christianity's place among other world religions. "I call myself a Christian," he confessed, "because my relation to God has been, so far as I can see, deeply conditioned by the presence of Jesus Christ in my history and

---

[53]James M. Gustafson, interview with author, New Haven CT, 27 June 1972.

[54]HRN, *Purpose of the Church and Its Ministry,* viii.

[55]HRN, "Why Restudy Theological Education?" *Christian Century* 71 (28 April 1954): 517.

[56]HRN, *Purpose of the Church and Its Ministry,* 21-24.

[57]Ibid., 9-17.

[58]Ibid., 36-39.

in our history." Jesus Christ, he continued, was for him "the one who lived and died and rose again" for the sake of "bringing God to men and men to God" and of "reconciling men to each other and their world."[59] Still, he did not claim that God worked exclusively through Christ. The truth for which the Western church had long contended was that the Spirit of God also proceeded from the Creator and Father of all things. This, Niebuhr insisted, made the Christian point of view theistic rather than christocentric. Christians dared not restrict redemption to the sphere that only they understood. "When the principle of being is God," he declared, "then he alone is holy and ultimate sacredness must be denied to any special being. No special places, times, persons, or communities are more representative of the One than any others."[60]

In Niebuhr's view, future pastors needed to learn to see the "world" as more of a "partner" of the church. After all, both communities lived before God, and each possessed unique knowledge and actions that might contribute to the divine process of redemption.[61] For him, this perspective implied a more interdisciplinary approach to theological education. Separation from the humanities and secular sciences, he asserted, allowed theology to become self-centered and to exaggerate its own problems. "Interpenetration" served to develop a broader view, as when students learned to consider the role of pastoral counseling in light of the general demand in society for personal counseling and began to see how they might join professionals other than themselves in meeting it.[62]

The "world," as Niebuhr saw it, also called forth a new conception of the office of the ministry in the "church." He assigned it the somewhat bland title of "pastoral director." That title, he was convinced, would eliminate much of the confusion surrounding traditional models of the ministerial office. For one thing, it specified the goal toward which pastors were to direct all parish activities. While preaching, teaching, and counseling remained standard duties, the pastor's task in the performance of them all was to build up a "royal priesthood" of believers committed to the gospel and determined to bring it to bear on the local community and world. To him, every "pastoral director" was in fact a "minister" to a "ministering community" of Christians. This did not mean that pastors were to avoid involvement in the "world." On the contrary, it made

---

[59]HRN, *The Responsible Self,* 43-44.

[60]HRN, *Radical Monotheism and Western Culture,* 52.

[61]HRN, *Purpose of the Church and Its Ministry,* 25-27.

[62]HRN, "Isolation and Cooperation in Theological Education," *Theological Education in America* 3 (January 1955): 1-6.

congregations the ones responsible for ministering to the world, while the job of pastors was to equip and strengthen them for that task.[63]

Perhaps the most important plank in Niebuhr's reform platform was his support for an ecumenical movement that endeavored to serve the "world" as much as the "church." For him, Jesus Christ had not only reconciled Christians to each other, but the whole of heaven and earth to the one sovereign God. This monotheistic impulse dethroned all other absolutes and rival faiths and affirmed the potential for good in every aspect of God's creation. It also kept pushing Christian definitions of "neighbor" beyond the boundaries of the church and demanded that Christians include all companions in the realm of being, enemy as well as friend, animal and inorganic as well as human.[64]

Niebuhr's writings implied that there were actually two ecumenical movements. He called the one "visible" ecumenism; it was distinctly Christian and saw the organization of church councils and federations, the union and reunion of denominations, as the best way to achieve a more ecumenical church. "Invisible" ecumenism, on the other hand, was more of a spiritual phenomenon. It expressed the longing of humankind in general for community, reflected the work of the Holy Spirit who proceeded as much from the world's Creator God as the Son, and thus transcended Christianity and the unity of its churches. It viewed multiple churches as representing different talents, all of which had the potential of contributing something to world unification.[65] To Niebuhr, both ecumenical movements were important. But ecumenical institutions were "justified" only by "the grace of God," which used them "beyond all our own conscious and unconscious intentions" to unite the total society and world.[66]

5

Similarly strong was Niebuhr's effort to create a "living tradition" in theology, one that kept past and present in proper tension. To see this, we need only to take a close look at the approach to Christian ethics he outlined in lectures published after his death in 1962 as *The Responsible Self.* An "ethics of responsibility" was the name he used to distinguish his position from other ethical theories. He viewed morality as neither a set of rules nor the choice of desired ends, but as dialogue conducted with other moral agents holding the same interpretive scheme to determine the fitting response to actions upon oneself. For Christians, this meant that the divine indicative they perceived

---

[63]HRN, *Purpose of the Church and Its Ministry,* 48-94.

[64]HRN, *Radical Monotheism and Western Culture,* 31-37.

[65]See HRN, *The Churches and the Body of Christ* (Philadelphia, 1953) 3-12; "The Seminary in the Ecumenical Age," 300-10.

[66]HRN, "The Seminary in the Ecumenical Age," 306-307.

with the aid of God's revelation as Creator, Governor, and Redeemer of the universe always determined the moral imperative. Niebuhr believed that the biblical record tended to support this approach. Isaiah's prophetic counsel to Israel was a call to see the "intentions of God" in the actions of their enemies. Also, the God to whom Jesus pointed in the New Testament was in fact the "doer of small and of mighty deeds," the meaning of which could be discerned by those who knew "how to interpret the signs of the times." Barth's perspective, on the other hand, reflected an emphasis on "right believing" and followed the "deontological" pattern that made morality a matter of strict obedience to a fixed set of principles.[67]

Niebuhr's approach allowed no one to prescribe the "fitting" response to every moral dilemma. He felt that each response needed to be worked out through conversation with others and, above all, in view of what God was doing in the particular situation. God's revelation might indeed suggest similarities between the Manchurian crisis and World War II; Niebuhr viewed both as the judgment of God on the self-interested policies of nation states. Yet the responses he considered most appropriate for each of these situations were clearly different. While repentance in the case of Manchuria meant detachment from the imperialism reflected in Japan's behavior, it summoned the United States during World War II to protect weaker nations from their totalitarian oppressors.[68] This may also be the reason Niebuhr's critics have tended to focus on his reluctance to give a more specific content to his ethics.[69] Niebuhr, it seems, was only following his own "reformation" principle and allowing for the freedom to deal creatively with every new situation.

Conversely, such obvious aversion to religious dogmatism never implied an existential relativization of all truth. Nor was his "ethics of responsibility" the equivalent of "situation ethics." In his eloquent "Concluding Unscientific Postscript" to *Christ and Culture,* Niebuhr admitted that his thinking was fragmentary and related to time, place, and values that were as relative as those of any other human being. For this reason, none of his five models provided the completely "Christian" answer to the question of the church's proper relationship to the world. Yet he insisted that the basis of all knowledge was not "relativistic." It still assumed an "Absolute" to whom Christians in faith might look for guidance. It also called forth a decision. Every person, Niebuhr went on to say, stood within a community and arrived at decisions through dialogue with others that always took place within the even larger context of history. In de-

---

[67]HRN, *The Responsible Self,* 47-68.

[68]Compare HRN, "The Grace of Doing Nothing," *Christian Century* 49 (23 March 1932): 378-80, and "War as the Judgment of God," ibid. 59 (13 May 1942): 630-33.

[69]See Lonnie Kliever, *H. Richard Niebuhr* (Waco TX, 1977) 145-50.

cision making, one might seek a "present" confrontation with Christ. Yet the Christ whose historic incarnation had given all time the potential for revelation made consultation with persons from the church's past just as necessary.[70]

Niebuhr's death in 1962 prohibited him from gaining a longer perspective on the postwar period and the reasons for the waning of the "return to religion" that had registered so forcefully on a variety of institutional scales. Yet even now his views remain amazingly enduring and prophetic. The revival's fundamentalist and neoorthodox elements alike, as he saw it, were as flawed by human idolatry as any other aspect of American culture. Both gave a part of the Christian heritage the reverence only God deserved to command. Ecumenists, on the other hand, forgot that denominational institutions possessed the capability of not only thwarting, but expressing the true aims of the church; and they tended to identify Jesus Christ too exclusively with the divine plan of redemption. The "transformation" of culture for Niebuhr implied determination on the part of churches to maintain a monotheistic focus in all their affairs, to make the "world" as well as the "church" the objective of Christian unity, and to engage in a theological process that kept tradition in tension with contemporary concerns.

---

[70]HRN, *Christ and Culture,* 230-56.

Epilogue

Richard Niebuhr was a man for whom the vocation of churchman remained central throughout his life. Reared in a Midwestern parsonage, he followed his father into the ministry of the Evangelical Synod of North America. There he served faithfully, first as pastor and then as a teacher and administrator at both Elmhurst College and Eden Seminary. In his estimation, the synod had allowed its "Germanness" to isolate its churches from the mainstream of American culture. The type of training it gave him and members of his generation reflected the religion of the Old World more than the New, thus requiring him to round out his education in the graduate schools of American universities. World War I broke some of the denomination's ties with German culture. Nevertheless, Niebuhr believed that it remained too narrow in its outlook and too small in size to make any real contribution to the larger world around it. Throughout the 1920s, Niebuhr stood in the forefront of those who sought to renew the ecumenical impulse of the synod's earlier years. His teaching at Eden aimed to inculcate a larger vision of religion and culture. When he became president of Elmhurst, that aim was the hallmark of the policies he initiated. The deep sympathy he preached for any human effort to realize God's kingdom on earth helped to broaden the synod's stand on the social issues of the day and brought him the chairmanship of the Evangelical delegation that eventually negotiated the "organic union" with the Reformed church. At the same time Niebuhr saw pitfalls in the process of acculturation. Exposure to the sociology of Ernst Troeltsch and Max Weber showed him the extent to which political, economic, and racial differences were mirrored in church structures and thus tended to alienate the working classes from America's old-line denominations. He described these differences with considerable emotion in *Social Sources of Denominationalism.* As a necessary step toward the revitalization of a flagging Protestant establishment, he prescribed a "withdrawal" of the church from the world.

Theologically, Niebuhr took issue with the liberal identification of Christianity with cultural progress and eschewed its optimistic assessment of human nature. He showed little sympathy for those who interpreted the Christian faith in dogmatic rather than historical terms. As a result, conservative elements in the Evangelical Synod at times found his view disturbing. As much as Karl Barth and those who subsequently formed the neoorthodox movement, however, he insisted on the transcendent reality of God. So, during the decade of the 1930s, the balance of Niebuhr's concern for Protestantism in general tipped toward a Christ-against-culture position. He returned from a sobering trip to Europe in 1931 only to witness the grim tide of the Depression now engulfing American life. To him, the economic and political chaos that came in its wake was God's way of bringing people to their knees in repentance. Especially in *Church Against the World,* he called for renewal of faith in a sovereign God. He asserted that this meant repudiation of the idolatrous aspects of such ideologies of the modern world as capitalism, and suggested that such action might involve detachment on America's part from the politics of self-interest. After joining the faculty of Yale Divinity School, Niebuhr also contended that hard times had come upon the social gospel because the twentieth-century phase of the movement tended to ignore the stark realities of human sinfulness and to become almost completely identified with liberal Protestantism. The new generation of leadership had forgotten what Jonathan Edwards knew too well, that "true virtue" required that God first accomplish a "second birth," a conversion of the human heart and will. Niebuhr's intention was not to condemn the social gospel, but to transplant it back into the soil of that evangelicalism from which it had first emerged in the nineteenth century. Then, as he proposed in *The Kingdom of God in America,* Christians would learn to love their neighbors not because of the intrinsic worth of the human personality, but because they were creatures of God and sacred by virtue of their relationship to the one whom Jesus Christ had shown to be seeking their redemption.

Additional concerns over the church and its role in the world were triggered by the outbreak of World War II. Niebuhr knew that church leaders dared not repeat the mistake of World War I, when they gave their unqualified blessing to America's cause. On the other hand, the isolationist-interventionist debates prior to Pearl Harbor convinced him that to stay aloof from the political process was just as unthinkable. He felt that the church must both declare God's judgment on the nationalist aspects of the conflict and work for a peace that conformed to the redemptive outcome God was accomplishing for enemy as well as ally. Such thinking led Niebuhr to reject the position he later identified as "Christ and culture in paradox." Those who espoused it during World War II tried to separate civic duty from the realm of Christian responsibility. To him, this implied not only a double standard, but a dualistic point of view that diminished the sovereignty of God and permitted the deification of values like "democracy." The Christian faith, as he saw it, was a form of "radical monotheism." The revelation of God to which it pointed exempted no aspect of culture from "conversion." The name Niebuhr assigned to this type of outlook was "Christ the transformer of culture." In response to developments that shaped the Cold War era in America, he clearly embraced that option.

During the 1950s Niebuhr channeled his earlier concerns into a vision of church renewal. On the one hand, his writings reverberated with criticisms of the postwar revival that was sweeping America's churches. To him, modern Protestantism was culpable because, like medieval Catholicism, it tended to identify God with religious institutions and doctrines. Fundamentalist groups kept confusing the authority of the Bible with the authority only its Author deserved to command. Barthians, on the other hand, concentrated so much on the doctrine of Christ that they tended to diminish the lordship of God. While supporting ecumenism, Niebuhr felt that its leaders, partly as a result of exalting the importance of their own affairs, gave excessive attention to the church. As a theologian, he also put more distance between himself and the "dead traditionalism" of neoorthodoxy and grew more appreciative of liberalism's efforts to reformulate Christian beliefs in light of contemporary thinking. However, it was in his capacity as director of a major study of theological schools throughout North America that he chose to set forth the reforms inspired by his contention that "conversion" was a process in which the church—as much as the world—must involve itself.

In fact, Richard Niebuhr's career drew to a close much as it had begun within the Evangelical Synod of North America. In 1960 he was called on to give a major address at the inauguration of James I. McCord as president of Princeton Theological Seminary. Published shortly thereafter in *Theology Today,* his "Seminary in the Ecumenical Age" embodied the rich and balanced thinking of a theologian who had given a lifetime to reflection on the "church" and the "world." Less obvious was its continuity with a position he had taken much earlier. Indeed, Niebuhr's central theme was the same one he had set forth nearly forty years before in his "Sociological Interpretation" of Eden Seminary. As in 1922, he applauded the "common mind" that ecumenical movements were helping to develop among Christians, but again emphasized that such efforts were always penultimate to the creation of one world through the reconciliation of the whole of humanity. This goal could not be achieved if the church were not "more fully reconciled with itself." Yet Christ, he stated, "reconciled us not to himself or to one another first but to the maker of heaven and earth, to the sovereign power by which and in which all things are"; he "sends his Church into all that world, charging it with the ministry to reconciliation."[1]

---

[1]H. Richard Niebuhr, "The Seminary in the Ecumenical Age," *Theology Today* 17 (October 1960): 307.

INDEX

Biog. 230.0924 N-d 117587

Diefenthaler, Jon.

H. Richard Niebuhr